A STUDY GUIDE

FOR

JOSEPH RATZINGER'S
(POPE BENEDICT XVI)

JESUS
OF NAZARETH

PART TWO: HOLY WEEK FROM THE ENTRANCE INTO JERUSALEM TO THE RESURRECTION

Foreword by
Timothy Gray, Ph.D.

Introduction by
Mark Brumley

Outlines and Questions by
Mark Brumley, Curtis Mitch, and Laura Dittus

Summaries and Glossary Terms by
Mark Brumley and Curtis Mitch

IGNATIUS PRESS   SAN FRANCISCO

Cover art (left):
Christ's Descent from the Cross
and
Cover art (right):
Christ's Appearance Behind Locked Doors
The Maestà Altarpiece
Painted 1308–1311 for the Cathedral of Siena
by Duccio di Buoninsegna
Museo dell'Opera Metropolitana, Siena, Italy
© Scala/Art Resource, New York

Cover design by Roxanne Mei Lum

© 2011 by Ignatius Press, San Francisco
All rights reserved
ISBN 978-1-58617-605-1
Printed in the United States of America ∞

Contents

Foreword

The Second Vatican Council's Dogmatic Constitution on Divine Revelation, *Dei Verbum* (The Word of God), outlined the essence of a Catholic approach to Scripture as combining both history and theology. On the one hand, the Council emphasized the importance of studying the historical context of Scripture for understanding the meaning intended by the human author of a particular text of Scripture. This means literary genre, social context, and understanding of ancient languages and cultures must all be taken into account to best understand the text of Scripture within its historical context. On the other hand, since the human authors were inspired by the Holy Spirit, one must also be sensitive to the divine Authorship at work in Scripture. Thus, although the Bible is made up of seventy-three different books, by numerous authors (sixty-six books in the Protestant Bible), over a long period of time, it must still be understood within the context and unity of God's plan. This approach, now often referred to as canonical exegesis, will be important for Pope Benedict's approach to Scripture, since it contains a record of Jesus' words and deeds. This theological dimension of Scripture must also be read within the living Tradition of the Church and according to the analogy of faith. In other words, Scripture is to be read within the Church, a vital point that Pope Benedict has repeatedly made.

History and Theology

Indeed, both of these methodological approaches, the historical and the theological, are seen as essential in Pope Benedict XVI's post-synodal apostolic exhortation on Scripture, *Verbum Domini* (The Word of the Lord). In a sense, history and theology are the two ears by which we must hear, in stereo, the word of God. For Vatican II and Pope Benedict, history and theology are the two legs upon which a proper exegesis must stand—neither leg can stand alone. Thus, Benedict observes in *Verbum Domini* that "only where both methodological levels, the historical-critical and the theological, are respected, can one speak of a theological exegesis, an exegesis worthy of this book" (*Verbum Domini* 34; hereafter abbreviated *VD*). Just as faith and reason are the two wings by which we ascend to God (according to Pope John Paul II's encyclical on faith and reason, *Fides et Ratio*), so too, history (reason) and theology (faith) are the two wings by which we are to ascend to an understanding of God's word.

It is worth noting that volume two of *Jesus of Nazareth* is the first major work of Benedict after his outline of the key principles of Catholic biblical interpretation given in *Verbum Domini*. One of the striking features of *Jesus of Nazareth, Part Two* is his modeling, rather consciously, of how a Catholic scholar should read Scripture. Indeed, in his preface, he notes that the historical-critical hermeneutic (approach to reading Scripture) should be combined with the theological approach, which is the "art" of reading the Bible that needs to be recovered. He goes on to say that "fundamentally this is a matter of *finally* putting into practice the methodological principles formulated for exegesis by the Second Vatican Council (in *Dei Verbum* 12), a task that unfortunately has scarcely been attempted thus far" (*Jesus of Nazareth, Part Two*, p. xv, emphasis added). Note the rather strong words, "finally" and "scarcely". Attending to both the historical and theological dimensions of Scripture together is something that, in the Pope's mind, is rarely being done. This, in short, is the methodological aim of his book on Jesus; for in addition to his desire to search the face of God in Jesus and thus bring a deeper reflection upon the figure of Jesus, his other aim is to model this rare art of combining history and theology, in his study of the Word made flesh.

Thus, my aim in this foreword is to walk through the principles of Catholic interpretation that the Pope outlines in *Verbum Domini*, and show how he practices what he preaches in his second volume of *Jesus of Nazareth*.

History

In *Verbum Domini*, Pope Benedict mentions that although the historical and theological approaches, or hermeneutics, are distinct, they should not be separated or opposed. He warns of a "sterile separation" that is often present in historical methodology, when it is cut off from theology (*VD* 35)—such isolation of historical and rational methods of study from theology and faith stems from a "positivistic and secularized hermeneutic ultimately based on the conviction that the Divine does not intervene in human history" (*VD* 35). This narrow methodological approach, which often handicaps historical critics, is precisely the flawed method that the Pope critiques in his preface to volume two of *Jesus of Nazareth*, where he singles out the "positivistic hermeneutic", which itself is "a specific and historically conditioned form of rationality that is both open to correction and completion and in need of it" (*Jesus of Nazareth, Part Two*, pp. iv–xv). The problem is not history, but rather the philosophical presuppositions that too often undergird how historical methods are employed and viewed. In other words, an exegete who reads Scripture using historical methods with the philosophical notions that there is no God who exists or who enters history will likely conclude that the divine and supernatural elements of Scripture are not historical.

In reaction to such errant conclusions some have turned against history and reason and have wanted to read the Bible by faith alone. Such a fundamentalist approach, however, is rightly condemned; it is not wrong in affirming the place of faith, but rather in its throwing out of reason. Unfortunately, those in the academic world who seek to shut out faith all together also often condemn the pursuit of combining reason with faith as a fundamentalism. This rationalism, however, which seeks "reason alone", is just as flawed as the fundamentalist who seeks "faith alone". Benedict's critique of this approach is seen in his concluding remarks on the meaning of Jesus' atoning death, saying that too often exegetes exclude the theological dimension of atonement, and thus he warns that "the mystery of atonement is not to be sacrificed on the altar of overweening rationalism" (*Jesus of Nazareth, Part Two*, p. 240). Thus, in response to the strident secularism that seeks a separation from faith, Benedict argues in *Verbum Domini* that the "true response to a fundamentalist approach is the faith-filled interpretation of sacred Scripture" (*VD* 44).

The Catholic, and balanced, position is one that combines faith and reason with history and theology. History, properly done, can lay the foundation for deeper theological understanding. For example, Benedict cites the German scholar Joachim Jeremias' historical examination of Jesus' address of God in his Gethsemane prayer as "Abba, Father". Observing that in the Jewish mind of Jesus' day such address was reserved for a child speaking to his father, Jeremias notes that such address to God would be seen as disrespectful, but yet it marks out a unique feature of Jesus' identity and prayer. Jesus spoke to God like a child to his father. This intimacy of address reveals the inner mystery of the figure of Jesus for Benedict and opens a reflection on Jesus' filial relation to God. This theological reflection builds upon the historical understanding of the uniqueness of such prayer in Jewish practice. Here we see, in Benedict's analysis of Jesus' prayer in Gethsemane, how historical understanding can lead to and deepen the theological meaning of the text.

Redaction Criticism

One element of historical-critical methodology that Benedict often refers to is redaction criticism. This method seeks to identify where sayings and traditions of Jesus have been edited and refined by the author of a Gospel. Do such redactions or differences between authors mean that the Gospels cannot be trusted? Certainly not! As Benedict observes while treating of the various accounts of Jesus' trial in Matthew, Mark, Luke, and John, none of them are giving us a transcript or recording of what exactly was said, but they do give us the truth of the essence of what was said and done. Indeed, from a historical perspective the various Gospel accounts of Matthew, Mark, Luke, and John help give credibility to the historical truth of the Church's faith in Jesus since they provide multiple witnesses. Indeed, if the four witnesses agreed in every detail it would cast suspicion that there was collusion, rather than complementary testimony.

Redaction criticism brings to our attention, for example, that Matthew typically has Jesus proclaiming the "kingdom of heaven", whereas Luke prefers "kingdom of God", and then asks the question "Which did Jesus say?" The answer is that "heaven" is a Jewish circumlocution for "God", and Matthew has in mind a more Jewish audience, while Luke, as a Gentile, translates the circumlocution to its literal meaning—"kingdom of God"—for his Gentile audience. The words are different but the meaning is the same. Ancient Greek historians such as Thucydides and Polybius even speak of how when the historian records speeches he must not make them up but rather word the accounts according to what was truly said. The wording may not be exact—indeed, it often will reflect the literary and theological tastes of the author—but it must be faithful to the historical words and deeds. Redaction criticism, therefore, notes the way different authors select and word their accounts. Benedict employs this method throughout his study, noting the different wordings of the Gospel narratives, but highlighting how they are similar in essentials.

Benedict makes this point when examining the four accounts of Jesus' institution of the Eucharist at the Last Supper, comparing Matthew, Mark, Luke, and Paul's account (in 1 Corinthians 11:23–26); he notes that "the four accounts are very similar in essentials, yet there are differences in detail that have understandably received a great deal of attention in exegetical literature." Benedict believes that although the accounts differ in detail, they are all true and authentic. "At the same time," Benedict observes, "accuracy of transmission does not exclude a degree of concentration and selection" (*Jesus of Nazareth, Part Two*, pp. 115, 117). In other words, Luke or John may be selective in their accounts of what Jesus said and did, with an eye to the pastoral needs of their community to whom they are writing—they are simply shaping and framing what Jesus really did and said.

Here we see the striking balance that Benedict proposes for Christians who interpret Scripture. On the one hand, they need to use their reason critically, noting the differences in detail between the Gospel accounts, aware of how sayings and events are passed on by oral tradition, while on the other hand firmly trusting in the authenticity, truth, and accuracy of these various accounts. In this way, Benedict hopes to show the Gospels and Christian interpretation to be both credible and realistic. "The important thing for us, then, is to ascertain whether the basic convictions of the faith are historically plausible and credible when today's exegetical knowledge is taken in all seriousness" (*Jesus of Nazareth, Part Two*, p. 105). Faith and reason along with history and theology should not be in tension but in unity—this is what Benedict is at pains to teach and model in this book.

Theological Exegesis: Three Principles

Given the central claim of Christianity, that God entered history and became man in the person of Jesus, there is no avoiding history for serious-minded Christians. This is why Benedict is passionate about the importance of reason and history in understanding Jesus and the Scriptures. Yet, the Bible cannot be reduced to the writings of men or to the past alone, which is the object of historical study. Without its theological dimension, the Bible becomes just another human book, which is something that Benedict warns biblical scholars against doing in *Verbum Domini* (35). The next necessary step, for Benedict, is faith which holds to the divine Authorship of Scripture, which means that the words of Scripture are not locked in the past but have present meaning for us today, for God's word is living and active.

Reason is necessary, but it alone is not sufficient for our reading of Scripture. We must read Scripture within the living Tradition and teaching of the Church, for the Holy Spirit, which guides that Tradition and teaching, is imperative if we are to comprehend the mind of God and therefore the theological dimension of God's word. In *Verbum Domini*, Benedict speaks of three criteria for such a spiritual or, as he prefers to call it, theological reading, all of which are drawn from Vatican II's document *Dei Verbum* (12).

Canonical Approach

The first principle of reading Scripture in light of its divine Authorship is that of content and unity, which Benedict identifies with canonical criticism. There is, given the unity of God's authorship of Scripture, a unity to all of the seventy-three books of the Bible; they form, so to speak, one book. In *Verbum Domini* Pope Benedict cites Hugh of Saint Victor as a guide to this vital point: "All divine Scripture is one book, and this one book is Christ, speaks of Christ and finds its fulfillment in Christ" (*VD* 39). If, therefore, all of Israel's Scriptures are pointing to Jesus, we must read Jesus' words and deeds in light of the Scriptures of Israel. This is one of the major characteristics of Benedict's reflection on Jesus throughout this second volume.

A good example of this is Benedict's depiction of Jesus as a suffering servant. Here, Jesus not only takes on the Suffering Servant of Isaiah but for Benedict he also embodies David, another type of suffering servant of God. This is best seen in how Jesus takes up the Psalms, especially Psalm 22. In the canonical Psalter, David is the primary author of the Psalms, and "he thus appears as the one who leads and inspires the prayer of Israel, who sums up all Israel's sufferings and hopes, carries them within himself, and expresses them in prayer" (*Jesus of Nazareth, Part Two*, p. 146). In light of this ancient biblical tradition, Benedict, with the Christian tradition, sees Jesus as the new Davidic king, suffering on behalf of his people. This theological connection between David's and Jesus' royal suffering sets up Benedict's understanding of Jesus' death as an expiation for Israel.

Living Tradition

The second theological principle for reading Scripture fully is reading it within the living Tradition of the Church. Benedict does this through the rediscovery of the Church Fathers which permeates his work, as well as his references to how the Church's liturgy provides a normative tradition for reading the Bible. For example, in treating of Jesus' Palm Sunday procession into Jerusalem, Benedict explains the meaning of this event for us today by drawing on the Church's liturgical practice. "The early Church, then, was right to read this scene as an anticipation of what she does in her liturgy" (*Jesus of Nazareth, Part Two*, p. 10). Citing the *Didachē*, Benedict shows that the earliest Christian liturgy took up the *Benedictus* and Hosanna in acclaiming the eucharistic coming of Jesus in the Eucharist as the disciples hailed Jesus in Jerusalem. "For the infant Church, 'Palm Sunday' was not a thing of the past. Just as the Lord entered the Holy City that day on a donkey, so too the Church saw him coming again and again in the humble form of bread and wine" (ibid.). It is these kinds of deep spiritual reflections that make reading *Jesus of Nazareth, Part Two* so refreshing and rewarding.

Analogy of Faith

The third theological principle for reading Scripture according to God's divine Authorship is the analogy of faith, which means reading Scripture from the heart of the Church's faith. This principle presupposes that the God who inspired Scripture has also guided the Church in her official teaching, and that there cannot be a conflict between these two. Benedict sees the Church's teaching, from Councils to the *Catechism*, as a profound reflection on the meaning and truth of God's revelation given in Scripture, shaped and tested by the greatest minds and saints of the Church's history. To not avail one's self of this resource is to ignore the gift of knowledge God has given humanity.

A good example of reading Scripture according to the analogy of faith is Benedict's interpretation of Jesus' words at Gethsemane. "Nowhere else in sacred Scripture do we gain so deep an insight into the inner mystery of Jesus as in the prayer on the Mount of Olives" (*Jesus of Nazareth, Part Two*, p. 157). When Jesus prays "not my will but yours be done", Benedict examines the meaning of this prayer in light of what the early Church Councils have said about Jesus' human and divine nature in the Councils of Nicea and Chalcedon, while drawing on patristic authorities like Pope Leo the Great and the great Byzantine theologian Maximus the Confessor. Benedict's depiction of the drama of Jesus' human will submitting to God's is a profound reading of the Gethsemane narrative in light of the Church's teaching and Tradition. One could say that not only does Benedict stand on the shoulders of the saints and Doctors of the Church but his bracing analysis and reflection shows that he dances upon their shoulders, like David dancing before the presence of God in the Ark of the Covenant.

—*Timothy Gray, Ph.D., President*
Augustine Institute
Denver, Colorado

Introduction to This Study Guide

This study guide aims to help readers who approach *Jesus of Nazareth, Part Two* without the benefit of extensive theological or biblical training. The goal is to make the book more accessible and more fruitful, not to replace it.

Not a Work of the Magisterium

In *Jesus of Nazareth, Part Two*, Benedict XVI offers, as he did in Part One, a number of theological judgments and opinions about the life and teaching of Jesus, as well as how the Gospels should be interpreted. It just so happens that the author is the bishop of Rome, the Pope. How should readers understand the various judgments and opinions Benedict XVI offers in his book? Do they reflect "the teaching of the Catholic Church"?

Not as such. In other words, simply because Benedict takes a position on a theological issue in *Jesus of Nazareth, Part Two* does not mean that this position is "the teaching of the Catholic Church". Of course some of the things Benedict discusses are Catholic teaching. However, they are such for reasons other than that they happen to appear in *Jesus of Nazareth, Part Two*. They are taught elsewhere as official Catholic doctrine.

In Part Two, Benedict XVI does not spell out as he did in Part One (p. xxiii) that his theological opinions in the book are not an exercise of the Magisterium, the teaching office of the Catholic Church. He assumes readers know this. To be sure, he thinks the positions he presents in the book are true and compatible with Catholic teaching, but he wants readers to accept his positions on the basis of the arguments he makes for them, rather than on the basis of his authority as the bishop of Rome.

In other words, like Part One, Part Two is the work of a theologian who happens to be the Pope, not a document of the Pope of the Catholic Church. While Catholics are free to disagree with his arguments, they (and all other readers) should be willing to give due deference to the judgments of a scholar of Benedict's standing, as they would give deference to the judgment of experts in other fields.

How to Use This Study Guide

For each of the eleven sections of *Jesus of Nazareth, Part Two*—foreword, nine chapters, and epilogue—there is a corresponding section with (1) a summary of the section or chapter; (2) an outline; (3) questions for understanding; (4) questions for application; (5) a list of important terms; and (6) an area for readers to include their personal reflections on the reading. Also included in this study guide is a glossary of key terms.

The resources of this study guide can be used for individual study and reflection or for group study and discussion. Group study can easily be divided into eleven sessions, corresponding to the eleven sections of *Jesus of Nazareth, Part Two*. The following structure is recommended for each group session.

- Open with prayer
- Read aloud the chapter or section summary
- Discuss the summary
- Review and discuss the questions for understanding and application or discuss particular passages of the text
- Comment on personal reflection
- Close with prayer

Large numbers often pose problems for group discussion. Those interested in using this study guide with study groups may want to limit the group size to between three and twenty people. In parish settings, it might be helpful to create more than one study group.

We hope that through this study guide and through the work of Benedict XVI you may be led by the Holy Spirit to encounter Jesus Christ more deeply and evermore to "seek his face" (cf. Ps 27:8).

—Mark Brumley
President, Ignatius Press

※

The Foreword to Jesus of Nazareth, Part Two

Summary

The author is pleased to present Part Two of *Jesus of Nazareth*. He has been encouraged by leading exegetes to complete his work. He hopes that Protestant theologian Joachim Ringleben's *Jesus* (2008) can, along with his own work on Jesus, provide an ecumenical witness and serve the common task of Christians.

Benedict is grateful that the discussion of theological and historical methods of interpretation is becoming livelier. The German Catholic scholar Marius Reiser's recent book provides important guidelines for interpreting Scripture.

The historical-critical method has yielded what fruit it will. Scholarly exegesis (interpretation) must again see itself as a theological discipline as well as a historical one. It must recognize a properly developed "faith-hermeneutic" (interpretation of Scripture based on faith), which combines with a "historical hermeneutic" (interpretation of Scripture based on historical research) to form a complete method.

Combining the two approaches is an art to be remastered. Benedict hopes his work has taken a step in that direction. His method is that called for by the Second Vatican Council (*Dei Verbum* 12).

The guiding intention of his book was not to write a "Life of Jesus" or a book of Christology (the branch of theology concerned with understanding the person and work of Christ). Saint Thomas Aquinas' theological treatise on the mysteries of Jesus' life in the *Summa Theologiae* (*S. Th. III*, qq. 27–59) is closer to Benedict's intention. But Benedict's time and concerns explain why the structure of his book is different.

Benedict's goal is stated in the foreword to Part One: to present the figure and message of Jesus, the "real Jesus". This study could provide the basis for a "Christology from below", unlike the mainstream critical quest for the "historical Jesus", which winds up with too little to say about Jesus. Benedict has developed an approach to Jesus' words and actions in the Gospels that can lead to a personal encounter with the real Jesus.

Benedict's task is harder in Part Two. He avoids controversies over particular points and focuses on the essential words and deeds of Jesus. He uses the "hermeneutic of faith" as well as "historical reason", which he says is a necessary component of faith. He hopes he has been granted an insight into the figure of the Lord that can help all readers who seek to encounter and believe in Jesus.

This book focuses on the words and actions of Jesus himself; Benedict will try to address the subject of the infancy narratives (the Gospel accounts of Jesus' birth) in another work.

Outline

I. Presentation of Part Two of *Jesus of Nazareth*

A. Reception of the first volume, including encouragement from leading exegetes to complete the project

B. "Ecumenical companion" to *Jesus of Nazareth*: Joachim Ringleben's *Jesus*

II. Benedict's observations regarding the need for a new method of exegesis

A. Marius Reiser's book and its contribution to providing guidelines for new exegetical approaches

B. The fruit and limitations of the historical-critical method

C. Importance of the *combination* of both historical and theological elements of exegesis (faith hermeneutic and historical hermeneutic)

D. Benedict seeks to integrate these two methods in the present work and sees this method as putting into practice the exegetical method called for by the Second Vatican Council (*Dei Verbum* 12)

III. Guiding intention of the book

A. The intention was not to write a "Life of Jesus" or Christology

B. The intention is the same as *Jesus of Nazareth, Part One*: "to present 'the figure . . . and the message of Jesus'", the "real Jesus"

   1. Some similarity to Saint Thomas Aquinas' treatment of the mysteries of Christ's life in the *Summa Theologiae*, although the present book appears in a different context and has a different objective and structure

   2. This book combines the "hermeneutic of faith" and the historical hermeneutic to arrive at a "personal encounter" with Christ

   3. The greater difficulty of this task for Part Two is due to it covering the decisive sayings and events in Jesus' life

   4. The effort to avoid controversies over particular points and to focus on the essential words and deeds of Jesus

C. The infancy narratives did not fall within the realm of the present work; the intention is to provide a later treatment of this topic

Questions for Understanding

1. How does Benedict characterize the reaction of Martin Hengel, Peter Stuhlmacher, and Franz Mussner to Part One of *Jesus of Nazareth* (p. xiii)?

2. Pope Benedict refers to Joachim Ringleben's book *Jesus* as "an ecumenical companion" to *Jesus of Nazareth*. What similarities and differences does Benedict see between these two works (pp. xiii–xiv)?

3. Benedict points to the importance of a work by Marius Reiser. How does this work contribute to the discussion (pp. xiv–xv)?

4. What claim does Benedict make about the historical-critical approach to exegesis? What does he see that biblical scholarship needs to do to avoid "exhaust[ing] itself" and "becoming theologically irrelevant" (pp. xiv–xv)?

5. What does Benedict speak of as "an art that needs to be constantly remastered" (p. xv)? Does Benedict maintain that he has mastered this art in his present work? How does he relate the discussion of biblical exegesis to the method called for by the Second Vatican Council (p. xv)?

6. In presenting the intention of Part Two, Benedict begins by stating what it is not. To what does he compare and contrast his approach? What does Benedict state is the intention of Part Two (pp. xv–xvi)? Why did he decide not to include the infancy narratives in this volume (p. xvii)?

Questions for Application

1. How can Benedict's call for exegesis that combines both historical and theological dimensions assist me in the way that I read the Bible?

2. How can an understanding of Benedict's intention aid me in my reading of Part Two of *Jesus of Nazareth*?

3. How can I unite my intention in reading this work to the intention of Pope Benedict to help his readers encounter Jesus Christ?

Terms

Notes

CHAPTER ONE

The Entrance into Jerusalem
and the Cleansing of the Temple

Summary

Jesus enters Jerusalem before the Passover. John's Gospel mentions three Passovers during the ministry of Jesus; the Synoptic Gospels (Matthew, Mark, and Luke) consider only one Passover—the one of the final week of Jesus' earthly life. The geographical "ascent" of Jesus as he moves from the lower sea level of Galilee to Jerusalem represents an inner ascent of Jesus' self-offering on the Cross, and into heaven.

En route Jesus heals the blind Bartimaeus, who, along with the crowd, follows Jesus with the hope he is the "son of David", the Messiah. Jesus prepares to enter Jerusalem by requisitioning a donkey to ride into the city, as David's son Solomon did (1 Kings 1:33). This amounts to the claim to be a peaceful, humble king, not a warrior-conqueror (Zech 9:9). The crowd's response of Hosanna affirms their hope in Jesus as the Messiah.

The Hosanna of the crowd as Jesus enters Jerusalem anticipates the Hosanna of the sacred liturgy. The *Benedictus* of the liturgy ("Blessed is he who comes in the name of the Lord") recalls Jesus' humility as the liturgical action moves toward the Lord's coming in the humble form of bread and wine.

The day after Jesus enters Jerusalem, he drives out the money-changers and sellers in the Temple. Why? There are three main interpretations of Jesus' actions: (1) Jesus wants to reform the Temple practice; (2) Jesus is a political revolutionary, a Zealot; and (3) Jesus' own explanation for his actions: to recall the Temple's purpose as a house of prayer for all peoples and to reject the combination of worship and trade in the Temple. The final view is correct because Jesus wants to do more than reform the Temple and he rejects violence as the means of establishing God's kingdom.

Jesus' zeal is not that of a political revolutionary but of one who loves God's house. He quotes the prophet Jeremiah to show that the Temple of Jesus' time would meet the same fate as the Temple of Jeremiah's day: destruction. Through Jesus' death and Resurrection, he will become the new Temple in which people unite in the sacrament of Christ's body and blood. In this way, he will surpass and fulfill the Old Testament sacrificial system and render the Temple obsolete. The Resurrection of Jesus will bring a new way to worship God, not confined to any particular mountain—a worship in spirit and in truth (Jn 4:23).

Two incidents confirm that Jesus' cleansing of the Temple is no political revolt: (1) Jesus' healing of the blind and the lame in the Temple after he purges it (Mt 21:14) and (2) the Hosanna acclamation of the children in the Temple (Mt 21:15–16). Neither incident fits with the idea that Jesus was a political revolutionary.

Outline

I. **Entry into Jerusalem**

   A. Background to the discussion of Jesus' entry into Jerusalem for his final Passover

   1. Three Passovers during Jesus' ministry recounted in John's Gospel are condensed into one Passover in the Synoptic Gospels

   2. Jesus' pilgrimage to Jerusalem from Galilee involved a physical ascent that provides an analogue to his inner, spiritual ascent to the Temple, the Cross, and God's presence in heaven

   3. Jesus brings with him to Jerusalem a crowd of pilgrims and followers

   4. Crowd's hope in Jesus as the Davidic Messiah is bolstered by Jesus' healing of the blind Bartimaeus

   B. Jesus' preparations for his entry into Jerusalem reinforce his disciples' hopes he is the Messiah

   1. Jesus' royal claim and his entry into Jerusalem riding on a donkey

      a. Requisition of animals a royal prerogative

      b. Old Testament allusions implied by Jesus' entry on a donkey

         1) Genesis 49:10

         2) Zechariah 9:9

            a) Jesus as king of peace, not war, whose kingdom embraces the whole world

            b) The interpretation of this prophetic vision seen in retrospect

            c) Jesus makes a royal claim but he rejects the "Zealot" interpretation of the kingdom of God, as a kingdom built on violent revolt

   2. The setting or enthronement of Jesus upon the donkey alludes to Solomon's example (1 Kings 1:33)

3. The Messianic meaning, based on 2 Kings 9:13, of the spreading of the garments before Jesus by the disciples and the crowd

C. The Hosanna acclamation of the crowd of fellow pilgrims

1. The meaning of Hosanna (Ps 118)

2. The significance of Hosanna as an acclamation applied to Jesus

   a. Messianic overtones of the term in Jesus' time

   b. The crowd accompanying Jesus into Jerusalem is not the same crowd of people from Jerusalem who condemned him

3. The Hosanna of the children in the Temple

   a. Jesus' use of Psalm 8 to defend the children's Hosanna acclamations

   b. Background of Jesus' other encounters with children and their representation of humble littleness before God, which should be possessed by Jesus' disciples

   c. Children's Hosannas also point to Jesus' humble disciples

4. The Hosannas of Jesus' entry into Jerusalem anticipates the Hosanna of the sacred liturgy

   a. The *Benedictus* of the liturgy recalls Jesus' entry into Jerusalem, and his humility riding on a donkey points to his coming in the humble form of bread and wine

   b. The Hosanna also points to Jesus' coming now in the Holy Eucharist, in which he takes us up into his ascent to the Cross and Resurrection, to the definitive Jerusalem of heaven

II. The cleansing of the Temple

A. Jesus' action and his justification of it

1. Jesus entered the Court of the Gentiles section of the Temple and overturned the tables of the money-changers and buyers and sellers there

2. Jesus appealed to Isaiah 56:7 and Jeremiah 7:11 for justification

B. Three main interpretations of Jesus' action

1. Reform of Temple practice interpretation

   a. According to this view, Jesus' cleansing of the Temple was an attack on its abuse set by the Temple aristocracy, not on the Temple as such

   b. Pope Benedict's rebuttal: Jesus' words concerning the Temple go deeper than a mere reform of Temple practices

2. Political revolutionary interpretation

   a. According to this view, Jesus attempted to cause a political revolt and was arrested and executed for it

    b. Recent history of the theory, including the views of Robert Eisler and Samuel George Frederick Brandon, who held Jesus was a Zealot

    c. A short history of Zealotry

    d. Arguments for the view that Jesus was a Zealot and the recent decline of the view

    e. Pope Benedict's rebuttal

        1) Jesus' whole ministry and message reject violent political revolution: killing in God's name was not Jesus' way

        2) Jesus' zeal directed to a kingdom of peace, as indicated by his humble entry into Jerusalem as king of peace and slain servant who saves by his death, according to the prophecies of Zechariah (9:9) and Isaiah (52:13—53:12)

3. Jesus' own stated explanation

    a. Mark 11:17 includes two prophecies Jesus applied to his situation—the universalist vision of Isaiah 56:7 and Jeremiah's prophecy (Jer 7:11) about the Temple as a "house of prayer" rather than as a "den of robbers"

        1) Universalist vision of Jesus: God's house is to be one of prayer for all the nations to worship the God of Israel

           a) Commercial activity dominated in the Court of the Gentiles

           b) Jesus' cleansing of the Temple sought to remove barriers to common recognition and worship of Israel's God

           c) John's account of Palm Sunday: the Greeks who desire to see Jesus will "see" him when he comes close to all men in his crucifixion

        2) Jesus denounced the combination of worship and trade in the Temple by drawing on the language of Jeremiah (7:11)

           a) Jeremiah opposed the politicization of faith, whereby the rulers presumed God's protection because of the Temple

           b) John 2:19 indicates that the Temple's fate was bound up with Jesus' fate: his rejection and crucifixion led to the Temple's obsolescence because Jesus' risen body became the new Temple, which gathers people and unites them in the sacrament of his body and blood

    b. Jesus' zeal was not the political activism of the Zealots, but zeal for God's house (Ps 69:2–10), which led to Jesus' Passion

    c. True zeal for God is self-giving love

    d. Confirmation of the exegesis is found in two incidents in Matthew's Gospel

      1) The blind and the lame are healed by Jesus in the Temple (Mt 21:14); he is a healer, not a political revolutionary who destroys

      2) Children repeat the Hosanna acclamation in the Temple area (Mt 21:15)

Questions for Understanding

1. Jesus' ascent in physical elevation as he moved from Galilee to Jerusalem paralleled an "inner ascent" as he made his final pilgrimage to Jerusalem for Passover. What, according to Pope Benedict, was the "ultimate goal" of Jesus' ascent (p. 2)?

2. What event encouraged the crowd on the way to Jerusalem with Jesus to hope he was the new David, the Messiah (pp. 2–3)?

3. How did Jesus' obtaining a donkey and riding it into Jerusalem point to his kingship (pp. 3–6)? How do the Old Testament passages Benedict cites indicate the type of king Jesus envisioned himself as being (pp. 4–6)?

4. What does the pilgrims' acclamation of "Hosanna" tell us about their view of Jesus (pp. 6–9)? How are "Hosanna" and the acclamation "Blessed is he who comes in the name of the Lord" (the *Benedictus*), as used in the sacred liturgy, related to how the crowd used them during Jesus' entry into Jerusalem (pp. 10–11)?

5. What are the three main interpretations of Jesus' cleansing of the Temple (pp. 11–17)? What arguments does Benedict summarize for each view? Which interpretation does Pope Benedict favor (pp. 17–23)?

6. On what grounds does Benedict reject the view that Jesus was a political revolutionary (pp. 15–23)?

7. What two prophecies did Jesus combine to explain his actions in the Temple (pp. 17–18)? What was the purpose of the Temple's Court of the Gentiles (p. 17)? What links does Benedict see between Jesus' crucifixion and Resurrection, and the cleansing of the Temple (pp. 20–22)?

8. How does Benedict describe Jesus' "zeal" (pp. 22–23)? What is the "criterion for true zeal" (pp. 22–23)?

9. What are the two brief episodes that follow the cleansing of the Temple in Matthew's Gospel (p. 23)? What do these "announce" (p. 23)?

Questions for Application

1. Pope Benedict speaks of Christ's entry into Jerusalem as an "ascent". In light of Pope Benedict's discussion, how do we enter into the ascent to the heavenly Jerusalem, an ascent into God's presence through the Cross?

2. Christ's entry into Jerusalem provides us with many signs of his kingship. How can we better acknowledge and honor Christ's kingship in our daily lives?

3. How can an understanding of the background and varied meanings of the exclamation "Hosanna!" enrich my use of this prayer, especially in the sacred liturgy?

4. How can I become more childlike in order to offer "perfect praise" to God?

5. How can I practice the "true zeal" Jesus showed, the zeal that all Christians are called to have?

Terms

Notes

CHAPTER TWO

Jesus' Eschatological Discourse

Summary

Jesus' pilgrimage to Jerusalem provokes in him an expression of love and sorrow. Because he loves Jerusalem and longs for its conversion, he is sorrowful that it rejects his message of peace. He knows that Jerusalem is traveling the course to its own destruction, one that its inhabitants took when the Babylonians destroyed the Temple in 587 B.C. Jerusalem's Jewish leaders presumed that God would underwrite their political survival despite their failing to live up to the spiritual demands of the Covenant. Nevertheless, alas, it was not to be. Likewise, Jewish military efforts to overthrow the Romans would abysmally fail. The Temple's destruction by the Romans in A.D. 70 would be decisive: the sacrificial system of Judaism would cease.

The Temple's spiritual demise precedes its physical destruction. Both Jesus and the early Church affirm this truth. Despite Jesus' love for the Temple, he comes to regard it as a "deserted house". The time of the sacrifices according to the Law of Moses is over. Jesus himself is now the center of God's saving presence. His death on the Cross will be the definitive atoning sacrifice, which will fulfill the Old Testament sacrificial system. Christ—and his followers through their communion with him—will become the new Temple of God.

Jesus' eschatological discourse is probably the most difficult part of the Gospels to understand. Jesus refers to events that are in the future when he speaks of them but which have already happened by the time the Gospels are written. He also speaks of future events altogether beyond human experience, so his message is difficult to interpret. He frequently uses images and language drawn from Old Testament prophecy, which the people who transmit his sayings extend to their own situations, while keeping true to Jesus' original message. It is sometimes a challenge, then, to sort out what in Jesus' eschatological discourse applies to our past, such as the destruction of the Temple, and what applies to the future, that is, the end of the world.

Contrary to what a superficial reading of Jesus' message has led some commentators to believe, Jesus does say the end of the world will immediately follow the destruction of Jerusalem. He speaks of an interim "times of the Gentiles" in which the Church will proclaim the Gospel to the nations, in order for history to attain its goal. This interim time—the age of the Church—is not the full Messianic age, writes Benedict, but is a time of both suffering and hope. Meanwhile, Israel retains its distinct mission as a people set apart, until the "full number of the Gentiles" comes into the Church. Then, as Paul teaches in Romans 11:26, "all Israel will be saved".

Jesus speaks of the end of the world, but, as we have seen, he uses language taken from Old Testament prophecies—from the books of Daniel, Isaiah, and Ezekiel, among others. He uses standardized prophetical language in order to speak in perennial terms about the future. His words are thus always relevant. His followers can reread his message in light of their own circumstances, without his teaching involving "clairvoyant" descriptions of specific future world events.

But Jesus does not simply repeat the language of the Old Testament. He adds a new element: he identifies himself with the Son of Man figure from Daniel 7:13–14. He ties the cosmic events of the end of the world and of all human existence to himself. In this way, Jesus' apocalyptic teaching shows us how the word of God from the past illuminates our present and our future, including our future encounter of him as Judge of the living and the dead.

Outline

I. Background to Jesus' eschatological discourse

   A. Jesus' words of love and sorrow regarding Jerusalem

   B. Old Testament background of the protective, solicitous mother bird

   C. Jerusalem's rejection leads to its desolation

      1. Prophecies of desolation and divine abandonment: Jeremiah 12:7

      2. Parallel language from Josephus' reports of the final years before the beginning of the Jewish War

   D. Movement from language of desolation of the house of the Temple to its destruction in Jesus' eschatological discourse

   E. Eschatological discourse is probably most difficult text in the Gospels

      1. Difficulty of its context

         a. The discourse refers to Jesus' statements that include future events that were past events by the time the Gospels were written

         b. The discourse uses language that refers to further future events beyond time and our world of experiences

      2. Problem of the discourse's redaction history

         a. Jesus' language draws on images from prophetic tradition in order to point to realities beyond description

  b. Redactors could extend Jesus' language to their particular situations while remaining true to his message

 3. Not this book's task to enter into problems of redaction criticism and transmission history

II. Three aspects of Jesus' eschatological discourse explored in the book

 A. The end of the Temple

  1. Background to the destruction of the Temple and of Jerusalem in A.D. 70

   a. Why did Christians flee Jerusalem for Pella beyond the Jordan?

   b. What was the "abomination that makes desolate"?

   c. Some key events of the Jewish War and the destruction of the Temple

  2. Effect on Judaism of the end of the sacrifice and the destruction of the Temple

   a. Developments in Judaism as a result of the Temple's destruction

   b. The need to bring the Christian and Jewish ways of reading the biblical text into dialogue in order to understand God's will and his word

  3. The Christian reading of the end of sacrifice and the Temple's destruction

   a. Saint Gregory of Nazianzen's general statement about the temporary and transitional aspects of the old order of sacrifices

   b. Jesus' view of the Temple's demise

    1) Indisputable that Jesus foretold the Temple's destruction

    2) Jesus loved the Temple as his Father's, but Jesus knew its age was over with his death and Resurrection

   c. Early Christian interpretations: before the Temple was destroyed, it had already ceased its saving role in history, as a result of Jesus' death

    1) Jewish Christians' earliest approach:

     a) Meet for prayer in the Temple, but for "the breaking of bread" in their own communities

     b) Implicit shift from Temple sacrifices with the place of sacrifices now taken by the Eucharist

    2) Stephen and Paul

      a) Stephen, a "Hellenist": a Greek-speaking Jewish Christian

        (1) Jesus ended the era of the Temple and its sacrifice

        (2) Stephen is stoned to death; his trial and death resembles Jesus' Passion and death

      b) Paul

        (1) Paul's conflict over certain customs of the Law did not involve the Temple and its sacrifices

        (2) All the Old Testament sacrifices were fulfilled in the Cross of Christ

        (3) Romans 3:23: Jesus is expiation (*hilastērion*) for sins

          (a) Term for the covering of the Ark of the Covenant, where YHWH appeared in a cloud

          (b) Blood sacrifice of a bull was a sin-offering on the Day of Atonement to make up for lives of sinful men

          (c) Paul saw Jesus as the presence of the living God, whose sacrifices supersede the Old Testament theology of worship

          (d) Paul absorbed the Temple and its sacrificial theology into his Christology, so that for him the Temple was already "demolished" in Christ

        (4) Hebrews merely expands on what Paul developed from the earlier tradition of the Day of Atonement having been fulfilled in the Cross

B. The times of the Gentiles

  1. Read superficially, the eschatological discourse chronologically links the end of Jerusalem and the end of the world

  2. The eschatological discourse includes an interim period that Luke 21:24 calls the "times of the Gentiles"

    a. The Gospel of Luke seems uniquely to introduce the "times of the Gentiles" between the end of Jerusalem and the end of the world, but all three Synoptics recognize such an interim (Lk 21:24; Mt 24:14; and Mk 13:10)

    b. Paul also recognized an age of the Gentiles (Rom 11:25–26)

    c. The early Church mistakenly assumed this period would be relatively short, but the crucial point is that the disciples understood they had a mission to accomplish in this period

3. Missions of the Church and Israel in the "times of the Gentiles"

    a. In a sense, urgency of evangelization for the Apostles was due to the idea that the Gospel had to be taken to all nations in order for the world to arrive at its destiny

    b. Horrible misunderstandings of Israel's mission have weighed down our history, but beginnings of a correct understanding have been available to be rediscovered

        1) Bernard of Clairvaux's advice to Pope Eugene III not to try to convert the Jews because "the full number of the Gentiles" must first come into the Church, then Israel as a whole will be converted

        2) Hildegard Brem's interpretation of the above text as based on Romans 11:25

    c. Mission of the Church to evangelize the Gentiles during the "times of the Gentiles" is an essential element of Jesus' eschatological message

C. Prophecy and Apocalypse in the eschatological discourse

    1. Benedict's summary of the discussion thus far

    2. Some further points on the issues discussed in the summary

        a. The "times of the Gentiles" is not the full Messianic age, but one of suffering, yet with hope

        b. Several of Jesus' parables speak of the "time of the Church", so it is clear that Jesus' eschatology is not a purely imminent one

            1) Parable of the good and bad fish (Mt 13:47–50)

            2) Parable of the darnel in the field (Mt 13:24–30)

        c. Christians fled to Pella in Transjordan rather than fought to defend the Temple

            1) This corresponds to Jeremiah's approach during the Babylonian siege of Jerusalem (Jer 7:1–15; 38:14–28)

            2) Benedict quotes Gnilka on how Palestinian Christians did not participate in the Jewish War because they followed Jesus' teaching in the Sermon on the Mount

        d. Jesus' warning against false Messiahs and apocalyptic enthusiasm

            1) Jesus' message to be vigilant

            2) Paul's warning about Christian vigilance in 2 Thessalonians 3:10–12

e. Jesus' teaching about the persecution of his followers to come in the "times of the Gentiles" and the witness of suffering

3. The strictly apocalyptic section of the eschatological discourse

    a. Jesus spoke of the future largely in the language of ancient prophecy taken from the Old Testament books of Daniel, Isaiah, and Ezekiel

    b. This allows for a rereading of Jesus' words in light of new circumstances of history

    c. The new aspect of Jesus' use of prophecy: the Son of Man figure is identified as Jesus himself

        1) Cosmic events of the end of the world and our own futures are personally tied to Jesus, the Son of Man

        2) Jesus' word is more powerful and enduring than the entire universe (Mk 13:31), so that Jesus is the true firmament

    d. Jesus' use of Old Testament language to discuss the end of the world avoids tying his words to any specific time frame

        1) They do not involve "clairvoyance"

        2) They show us the right paths for today and tomorrow, without being limited to a specific time

        3) They prepare us to encounter him as the living Word and the Judge of all mankind

Questions for Understanding

1. Describe Jesus' attitude toward Jerusalem (p. 24).

2. How did the Temple's spiritual demise precede its physical destruction?

3. What are the central themes of Jesus' eschatological discourse (p. 26)?

4. Why is the eschatological discourse perhaps the most difficult text in the Gospels (p. 27)?

5. How is the Jewish War, which began in A.D. 66, relevant to our understanding of Jesus' eschatological discourse? (pp. 28–34)?

6. What reasons do Eusebius of Caesarea and Epiphanius of Salamis give for Christians' flight from Jerusalem before its siege (p. 28)? Identify a candidate mentioned by Benedict for the "abomination that makes desolate" (pp. 28–29). Why is this figure, whoever it was, significant for the early Christians? How does the flight of Christians from Jerusalem imply their rejection of a "Zealot" reading of the Bible (p. 29)?

7. What event occurred on August 5 in the year 70 (pp. 31–32)? How is this event key in salvation history (pp. 31–32)? What is the wider significance of this event for Judaism (pp. 32–33)? What are the two ways this event leaves for reading Scripture (p. 33)? What does Benedict XVI see as "our task" in relation to this (pp. 33–34)?

8. How does Saint Gregory Nazianzen understand the phases of religious history (p. 34)?

9. How did Christ view the Temple and its destruction (pp. 34–35)? What is "beyond doubt" in how Jesus spoke of the Temple (pp. 34–35)? What passages in Scripture speak of this (p. 35)? How does Benedict XVI depict Jesus' reverence for the Temple (p. 35)?

10. By the time of the Temple's destruction how had Christians come to think of its place in salvation history (p. 46)? How did Jesus bring about the Christians' thinking?

11. According to Benedict, why is it a mistake to think that Jesus held the end of the world would immediately follow the destruction of Jerusalem (pp. 41–43)?

12. What is the significance of the "times of the Gentiles" for the world's end (pp. 42–47)?

13. How does Saint Paul speak of the time of the Gentiles (pp. 43–44)? How did it make urgent his missionary preaching (pp. 43–44)?

14. How does Pope Benedict address the evangelization of Israel in this chapter (pp. 44–45)? Do his comments preclude any evangelization of Jewish people? What does he think about the ultimate destiny of Israel? What parables does Benedict point to as supporting the idea of an intermediary "time of the Gentiles" (p. 47)?

15. What attitude must the Christian have in light of "false Messiahs and apocalyptic enthusiasm" (p. 48)? How does Benedict define and characterize true vigilance here (p. 48)?

16. What is the significance of the Cross in the proclamation of the Gospel/end times (p. 49)?

17. What does Benedict speak of as the "strictly apocalyptic" part of the eschatological discourse (p. 49)? Why does Jesus draw so heavily on the Old Testament to speak of the end of the world and the judgment to come? What new, personal element does he add to his use of Old Testament language (pp. 50–51)? What does Benedict regard as the aim of the eschatological discourses (p. 52)?

Questions for Application

1. In what ways do I freely surrender to the loving, protective care of God (who cares for us as a hen cares for her chicks), and in what ways do I resist (to the point of perhaps risking my own destruction)? How can I submit myself to the Providence of God with a greater love and docility?

2. How can the destruction of the Temple in Jerusalem be seen as a sign of God's providence, leading us to Christ?

3. According to Benedict, there can come a point at which "ultimately, in the battle against lies and violence, truth and love have no other weapon than the witness of suffering" (p. 49). Have you seen the truth of this statement in your life? If so, explain how.

4. In what way is the period called the "times of the Gentiles" a time of evangelization? How do I share in this evangelical mission?

5. What does true vigilance entail (pp. 48–49)? How can I practice this virtue?

6. Is my worship of God one that is directed to the true Temple—the person of Jesus Christ—or does it have some other center (e.g., ego-centric, etc.)? How can I purify the intention of my prayer?

7. Read the last paragraph of this chapter (p. 52). How does this present a focus for reflection on the "end times"?

Terms

abomination that makes desolate, 28
Bernard of Clairvaux, 44
Brem, Hildegard, 45
Hellenists, 36
Jewish War, 25
Josephus, Flavius, 30
Mittelstaedt, Alexander, 29

Nazianzen, Gregory, 34
Pharisees, 24
Qumran, 33
times of the Gentiles, 42
Titus, 30
Torah, 32
Wilckens, Ulrich, 40

Notes

The Washing of the Feet

Summary

John's Gospel account of the Last Supper has two unique elements: Jesus' washing of his disciples' feet and Jesus' farewell discourses, including his "high-priestly prayer". Chapter three explores Jesus' washing of his disciples' feet; chapter four examines Jesus' high-priestly prayer.

Jesus' "hour" has come with the Last Supper. This "hour" is the time of his departure or stepping beyond this world (Greek, *metábasis*) to return to the Father. It is also the time of his great outpouring of self-giving and other-regarding love on the Cross (Greek, *agápē*). The latter is the way Jesus expresses his love for his disciples "to the end" (Jn 13:1; Greek, *télos*), meaning both the *end* of his life and the *end* in the sense of the goal to which his life and ministry have been directed. John's use of the Greek word for "end" (*télos*) anticipates Jesus' dying words "It is finished" (*tetélestai*), in the sense that the end or goal of his mission has been accomplished.

The language Jesus uses of "coming from" the Father and "returning" to him is similar to the language of the philosopher Plotinus. He and his followers espoused the idea of an *exitus* and *reditus*—an exit or "coming from" and a "return to". However, their *exitus* or "coming from" was a fall from divinity into the material world. Their *reditus* involved a return to the divine through purification from the material realm. For Jesus, his "coming from" the Father is not a *fall* but an act of *love* for man; his "return" to the Father is not a *purification* from the material realm but an *elevation* of humanity into union with God.

Jesus further expresses his humility by assuming the posture of a slave to wash his disciples' feet. This single act sums up his whole ministry. He divests himself of his divine splendor and washes our feet to make us fit to sit at God's wedding feast.

John's reference to Jesus' statement about the disciples being "clean" draws on the idea of "cleanliness" in the Old Testament and in world religions. Jesus transforms the notion of "purity": purity arises from the heart, not from ritual actions. Purity of heart also means more than moral reform; it comes from God's Spirit touching and transforming the heart through faith. Thus, neither ritual purity nor moral efforts purify us; the gift of the encounter with God through faith in Jesus Christ is what purifies us.

Plotinus' philosophy has man gradually purifying himself from matter and becoming spirit in order to ascend to God. Christianity has God-become-man making us pure and drawing us back to unity with God.

Jesus' act of foot-washing is both a symbol of his humble, others-regarding love expressed by his death *and* an example of how his followers should act. The Church Fathers used the terms *sacramentum* and *exemplum* to express these two aspects of Jesus' action. *Sacramentum* means the whole mystery of Christ's life and death, by which he unites himself to us and transforms us. *Exemplum* refers to the example Jesus sets, which we are to follow. The one leads to and enables the other. Christ's example becomes ours because he acts in us and enables us to follow him, not simply because we "copy" him.

Christ's "new commandment" is for us to love as he loves us. It is not new merely because it is a higher moral standard, but because it flows from our new way of existing as Christians—from God's gift of our *being-with* and *being-in* Christ. The Lord purifies our hearts so we can act in union with him as he acted. We are immersed in the Lord's mercy, and possess the grace of the Holy Spirit in us. We receive and live out the divine gift of new life. The gift (*sacramentum*) becomes an example (*exemplum*) we live, without ceasing to be a gift in us.

Judas and Peter represent two different human responses to Jesus' gift of himself for us. Judas betrays Jesus and falls into despairing remorse. Peter denies Jesus but repents.

At the Last Supper Jesus prophesies his betrayal. His words confuse the disciples, although John probably recounts Jesus' explanation more clearly than as Jesus originally gives it. Still, it is clear that some dining at table will betray Jesus.

John uses the Greek verb *trōgein* to translate Jesus' word for "eating". This linked the Last Supper to Jesus' teaching about the Eucharist in John 6:54–58, where the same Greek verb is used. Some later Christians also will betray Jesus even though they eat "his bread" of the Eucharist. In his "hour", Jesus takes upon himself his betrayal by Judas and by everyone else until the bitter end of history.

The evangelist gives no psychological analysis of the traitor; Judas simply succumbs to the domination of the devil. Afterward, he takes a single step toward conversion by admitting his sin. But his remorse turns into despair of divine forgiveness. In the end, he sees only darkness.

Unlike Judas, Peter falls but is healed through conversion. John 13 recounts two exchanges between Jesus and Peter that show how Peter falls into spiritual danger. First, Peter objects to Jesus washing Peter's feet. He does not think it appropriate for the Master to wash the feet of the disciple, nor is it something the Messiah would do. Second, Peter does not accept that Jesus would go to his death. Peter boasts that he would die to protect Jesus. Peter must learn that martyrdom for Christ is a gift of humility, not a heroic personal achievement.

Ultimately, both exchanges between Jesus and Peter are about not telling God what to do but accepting God as he reveals himself and then humbly allowing God to refashion oneself into true divine image.

Once Peter accepts that Jesus will wash his feet, he enthusiastically declares that Jesus should wash Peter's head and hands as well. Jesus gives an enigmatic reply that one who has bathed need only have his feet washed. The assumption is that the disciples already have bathed so that only their feet remain dirty from walking to dinner. However, John sees the deeper, symbolic meaning of Jesus' statement.

The "complete bath" Jesus presupposes is Baptism, which mysteriously "immerses" a man into Christ. Baptism is the action of the Lord in his Church, not man's own doing. Yet the Christian life requires ongoing cleansing in order to participate in table fellowship with the Lord. Foot-washing represents the acknowledgment of one's sins committed after Baptism. Christians need to confess their guilt and bring it into the light of Christ's purifying love in order for us to have "table fellowship" with him.

Jesus' act of washing his disciples' feet sums up his ministry as the servant of God who suffers for others. The second Suffering Servant Psalm (Is 49:3) anticipates John's theology of Jesus' Passion, which links suffering for God and glorifying him. In Jesus' abasement, God is glorified.

In John's account of "Palm Sunday", Jesus expresses the sorrow that the Synoptics indicate he also experiences in Gethsemane. As in Gethsemane, Jesus submits himself to carry out the Father's will on the Cross, in order to glorify him. The hour of the Cross is the hour of the Father and the Son's glory.

Outline

I. Introduction

   A. Benedict turns to the Fourth Gospel's account of Jesus' final evening with the disciples

   B. He postpones discussion of the differing chronologies of the Synoptics and John regarding the Last Supper

II. The hour of Jesus

   A. Two uniquely Johannine elements of the Last Supper accounts

      1. Jesus' washing of his disciples' feet and in this context his prophecy of Judas' betrayal and Peter's denial

      2. Jesus' farewell discourses and his high-priestly prayer

   B. With the Last Supper, Jesus' "hour" arrives—the essence of which involves two key words: *metábasis* ("departure") and *agápē* (selfless love)

      1. Jesus' "hour" is the goal of his ministry and the "hour" of his love that reaches to the end (*télos*)

2. John's use of *télos* at the Last Supper anticipates Jesus' final words on the Cross: *tetélestai*—"It is finished" (Jn 19:30)

C. Jesus' discussion of his coming from and return to the Father

1. Reminiscent of the philosophy of Plotinus, with its schema of *exitus* ("going out") and *reditus* ("return")

2. Differences between Plotinus' idea and Jesus' coming from and return to the Father

a. Plotinus' idea of "going out" is a fall from the divine into the material realm; his "return" is a purification from the material back into the divine

b. Jesus' "going out" is not a fall but an act of love for the creature; his "return" to the Father is an elevation of humanity, not its stripping away

D. Jesus' act of washing his disciples' feet is the act of a slave

1. The great Christological hymn of Philippians 2:7 points to Jesus' humility as a servant

2. The man Adam tried to grasp divinity; Jesus moved in the opposite direction, coming down from his divinity into humanity

3. Jesus' act of foot-washing represents his whole saving ministry in a single act: Jesus' self-giving "love to the end" cleanses us

III. "You are clean"

A. Jesus' use of term "clean" during his act of foot-washing

1. The concept of "cleanliness" in the Old Testament and world religions, which stresses cultic or ritual purification in order to approach the divine

2. Jesus' challenge to the notion of "cult purity" and purity of the heart

a. In Mark 7:14–23, Jesus insists that purity or impurity arises from the heart, not from ritual actions

b. Liberal exegesis has interpreted Jesus to mean purity arises from moral reform

c. But purity results from God touching men's hearts through faith

B. Jesus' later use, during his high-priestly prayer in John 17, of the related term "sanctification"

1. Jesus later discussed sanctification and consecration in the truth

2. "Consecration" means "to render fit for divine worship"

3. In John 13, it is the foot-washing that "cleanses"; it is the bath of Jesus' love to the point of death

4. Not ritual purity nor mere morality but the gift of encounter with God in Jesus Christ is what purifies

C. Contrast between Platonic philosophies of purification and Jesus' teaching

D. Jesus' purification and the worship through the new Temple of his body, the Church

IV. **Sacramentum and exemplum, gift and task: The "new commandment"**

A. Purity is the act and gift of God through his coming down to us and making us clean

B. Two opposing interpretations of the foot-washing, according to Schnackenburg

1. Foot-washing as a symbolic action pointing to Jesus' death

2. Foot-washing as a paradigm for ministry of the humble service of Jesus

C. Benedict rejects Schnackenburg's view that the second interpretation is an unrelated editorial addition; Benedict sees a unity of these views

D. The Fathers used the distinction between *sacramentum* and *exemplum*

1. *Sacramentum* here refers to the whole mystery of Christ in which he draws us close to him and transforms us

2. *Exemplum* is the example of Christ, which is no mere moral copying but a way in which Jesus' example becomes ours because he acts in us

E. The new commandment

1. What is not new about the "new commandment": not a new law or a new moral effort

2. What is new about the "new commandment": new foundation of being—being-with Christ and being-in Christ

   a. Augustine's shift in his exegesis of the Sermon on the Mount: from higher morality to a heart purified by the Lord

   b. Being immersed in the Lord's mercy

   c. Aquinas: new law is the grace of the Holy Spirit

   d. The gift (*sacramentum*) becomes an example (*exemplum*), without ceasing to be a gift

V. **The mystery of the betrayer**

A. Two different human responses to Jesus' self-gift: Judas's betrayal and Peter's denial

B. Judas' betrayal

   1. Jesus prophesied his betrayal

   2. The confusion of the disciples about Jesus' betrayal

   3. Jesus' comments were probably made clearer in John's account than they originally were for the disciples

   4. The main point: someone at the table would betray him

   5. John 13:18 uses the Greek verb *trōgein* for "eat", linking the Last Supper to the eucharistic teaching of John 6:54–58

      a. This anticipates the action of some later Christians who will traitorously partake of the Eucharist

      b. In his "hour" Jesus took on himself the betrayal of all ages

   6. John's interpretation of Judas

      a. No psychological analysis

      b. Judas allowed himself to come under diabolical dominion

      c. Judas' later remorse for his sin did not lead to repentance and forgiveness

         1) Judas' remorse turned to despair of salvation

         2) Judas came to see only himself in darkness

         3) John 13:30: Judas immediately departed from the Last Supper into the night—darkness

VI. Two conversations with Peter

A. Peter's denial: he fell but not permanently as Judas did

B. Two exchanges between Jesus and Peter

   1. Peter objected to Jesus' washing of Peter's feet

      a. It was against the master-disciple relationship and contradicted Peter's idea of the Messiah

      b. Throughout history others have held this view, but the Messiah passed through suffering into glory and leads others on this path

   2. The theme of true martyrdom

      a. Peter pledged his radical fidelity to Jesus in the face of Jesus' imminent death

      b. Peter had to learn that martyrdom is a grace of humility to be received, not a heroic personal accomplishment

   3. The two exchanges were about accepting God as he reveals himself and allowing oneself to be refashioned into his true image

VII. Washing of the feet and confession of sin

A. Jesus' enigmatic statement: one who has bathed need only have his feet washed

   1. Jesus assumed the disciples bathed before dinner so only their feet were dirty

   2. John brings out deeper, symbolic meaning of Jesus' words

   3. Foot-washing is not an individual sacrament but a *sacramentum*, or symbol of Jesus' whole saving, purifying ministry

   4. The "complete bath" occurred in Baptism, which is something the Lord does to us, not something we do for ourselves

   5. "Foot-washing" represents postbaptismal confession of sins in order to have table fellowship with the Lord

   6. Main point: sin should be confessed and brought into the light of Christ's purifying love for us to have table fellowship with him

B. Foot-washing and Jesus' role as Suffering Servant who glorifies the Father

   1. The foot-washing action summed up Jesus' ministry as servant of God suffering for others

   2. Second Suffering Servant Psalm (Is 49) anticipates John's theology of Jesus' Passion

      a. Jesus the Suffering Servant in whom God is glorified (Is 49:3)

      b. John's Palm Sunday account includes a kind of Johannine "Gethsemane", in which Jesus discusses his troubled soul but remains faithful to the Father's will (Jn 12:27–28)

   3. The "hour" of the Cross is the "hour" of the Father and the Son's glory

Questions for Understanding

1. When it comes to the dating of the Last Supper, how do the chronologies of the Synoptic Gospels (Matthew, Mark, and Luke) differ from the chronology of John's Gospel (pp. 53–54)?

2. What two events are unique to John's account of the Last Supper (p. 54)? Where does Benedict place the arrival of Jesus' "hour" (p. 54)? What two key words does Benedict say describe the essence of the "hour" (p. 54)? How are these two terms interconnected (pp. 54–55)? How do they help us to understand Jesus' "hour" (p. 55)?

3. Benedict refers to the themes of "coming from" (*exitus*) and "returning to" (*reditus*) (pp. 55–56)? How does Jesus' "coming from" and "returning to" the Father

differ from the philosopher Plotinus' ideas of *exitus* and *reditus* (pp. 55–56)? What new element do we find in Christ's return to the Father (p. 56)?

4. How is the foot-washing an example of "servant-love" (pp. 56–57)? How do Philippians 2:7–8 and Revelation 7:14 relate to the discussion of servant-love (pp. 56–57)?

5. What role do purification regulations play in world religions (pp. 57–58)? How were cultic purifications in the Judaism of Jesus' day viewed and what was Jesus' view of purity (pp. 58–60)? How does Benedict contrast the Christian concept of purity with that of the Platonic philosophies of late antiquity (p. 60)? With nineteenth-century piety's notion of purity (p. 60)? What does Benedict say about the passing away of Old Testament purification rituals (p. 61)?

6. How are we to see both a gift and task (*sacramentum* and *exemplum*) in the foot-washing (pp. 61–63)? How are these two things connected rather than being in conflict (pp. 61–63)? What is new about Jesus' "new commandment" (pp. 63–65)?

7. What two different responses to Jesus' gift does Benedict describe (p. 65)? On what three occasions does John's Gospel describe Jesus as "troubled" (p. 65–66)? What is common in these different instances (p. 66)?

8. What explanation is given for Judas' betrayal (p. 68)? What movement toward conversion do we see in Judas (pp. 68–69)? What is Judas' "second tragedy" (p. 69)? How does Judas exemplify "the wrong type of remorse" (p. 69)? What is true remorse (p. 69)?

9. How does Peter's fall contrast with Judas' (pp. 69–70)? What are two moments in John 13 where the danger of Peter's fall becomes visible (pp. 69–72)? What must Peter learn (pp. 69–72)? What do the two moments have in common (p. 72)?

10. How does Benedict explain the meaning of John 13:10 (pp. 72–73)? How does his interpretation relate to the issue of confession in the early Church (pp. 73–74)? What does Benedict say about the need for confession (pp. 73–74)?

Questions for Application

1. How can I practice the selfless *agápē*-love characteristic of Jesus' "hour"?

2. How does my life share in Jesus' *exitus* and *reditus*, his "coming from" and "returning to" the Father?

3. How can the discussion of purity and purification in this chapter help me better to appreciate the sacraments of Baptism and Confession?

4. In speaking of the connection between *sacramentum* (the gift of the mystery of Christ) and *exemplum* (the example and the task, or mission, that the mystery brings about), Benedict says that purity is a gift. Do I remember to ask for this gift? How do I live the task that purity calls for?

5. How can I identify myself with Peter's need to learn?

6. How can I imitate the servant-love of Christ? Do I place myself at the service of others?

Terms

agápē, 54
Augustine, 64
Barrett, Charles K., 66
exemplum, 62
Feast of Unleavened Bread, 53
high-priestly prayer, 54
hour of Jesus, 54
Knopf, Rudolf, 74
misericordia, 64
new commandment, 63

Pascal, Blaise, 68
Platonic philosophies, 60
Plotinus, 55
Prologue of John's Gospel, 56
sacramentum, 62
sacramentum futuri, 61
sanctification, 59
Schnackenburg, Rudolf, 62
tetélestai, 55
trōgein, 67

Notes

CHAPTER FOUR

Jesus' High-Priestly Prayer

Summary

Jesus' farewell discourses follow his act of foot-washing. The discourses culminate in what scholars call Jesus' "high-priestly prayer". The background of the Old Testament Feast of Atonement helps us understand this prayer.

According to Leviticus 16 and 23:26–62, on the annual Day of Atonement in ancient Israel, the high priest offered sacrifices for his own sins, those of the priestly caste, and those of the people of Israel. In this way, Israel's relationship as God's people was restored. The Covenant established this relationship. Later, the rabbis explained God's purpose in creating the world as providing a "space" for the Covenant to be established and lived. Sin disrupted this relationship and the Day of Atonement restored it.

Jesus' prayer in John 17 is based on the ritual of Leviticus 16. Jesus prays for himself, for his Apostles, and for all believers, as the high priest made atonement for himself, the priesthood, and all the people of Israel. In this way, Jesus shows that he is the high priest of the true Day of Atonement for the sins of the world.

Jesus' high-priestly prayer is the culmination of the Old Testament ritual of the Day of Atonement, as he transforms it into the Son's prayer to the Father. "Spiritual sacrifices", with worship shaped by the word and reason (Rom 12:1), replace animal sacrifices. The word of the "spiritual sacrifice" is the Word made flesh, who offers his body and blood. In this way, Jesus transforms his cruel death into "word"—the expression of his self-giving love. The new worship of Jesus' self-giving sacrifice is linked to the Eucharist.

The Suffering Servant image of Isaiah 53 prefigures the deepened image of the priesthood contained in Jesus' high-priestly prayer. The Suffering Servant "carries" the sins of others and offers himself as a "sin-offering". He is both the priest who offers and the victim offered in sacrifice. Although John 17 does not explicitly mention the Suffering Servant, John explicitly links Jesus to his role in John's account of Jesus' teaching about the Good Shepherd in John 10:11, 15, 17, 18.

Jesus' words and actions show outward discontinuity with the Temple's sacrifices, while he maintains a deep inner unity with the history of the Old Covenant and fulfills it.

Pope Benedict selects four principal themes from the wealth of material in John 17: (1) eternal life; (2) sanctification; (3) making God's name known; and (4) Jesus' prayer for unity among his followers.

(1) *Eternal Life.* Jesus' prayer includes the theme of life (Greek, *zōē*). Here, he refers explicitly to eternal life, which refers to "true" life from God, not only to the afterlife. Physical death affects only *bios* (ordinary life), not "true" life, or *zōē*. Man is intended for the life of *zōē*. He obtains it through "recognition" (which is a kind of union of being) with God, who is life. This "recognition" comes through faith in Jesus Christ, the one whom God has sent.

(2) *Sanctification.* Sanctification, or consecration, refers to the process of making a thing or a person holy. Only God is holy in the full sense of the word. Holiness of a thing or person means being "set apart" from the rest of ordinary life. It involves consecration for sacrifice or for priestly service in divine worship.

In John's Gospel, there are three sanctifications: (1) the Apostles are sanctified in the truth (Jn 17:19); (2) Jesus sanctifies himself (Jn 17:19); and (3) the Father sanctifies Jesus (Jn 10:36). The three sanctifications are explained, starting with Jesus' sanctification by the Father. The Father's consecration of the Son is identical to the Incarnation. As the Holy One of God, Jesus was united with the Father, and as a man, Jesus existed for the mission to the world, bringing the world back to God.

Jesus' self-consecration (Jn 17:19) means that he offers himself as high priest and as sacrifice for the world. The Jewish philosopher Philo anticipated the idea of the divine Word (Logos) as high priest, but Jesus made it concrete. As the Word made flesh for the life of the world (Jn 1:14; 6:51), he fulfilled the idea of the Day of Atonement.

The disciples are sanctified, or consecrated, in the truth (Jn 17:19). In Exodus 29:1–9, Aaron's sons were consecrated priests when they vested in sacred robes and were anointed. The Day of Atonement ritual refers to Aaron completely bathing before investiture with his sacred robe (Lev 16:4). The disciples of Jesus at the Last Supper are bathed in the truth and are invested with the robe of truth; the truth is Christ himself. Jesus' high-priestly prayer, then, includes the institution of the Apostle's priesthood, the New Testament priesthood.

(3) *Making God's name known.* Jesus is the new Moses, revealing God's name in a new and deeper way. The divine name was more than a word; it entailed God entering into communion with Israel and his being present in the midst of the people through their religious institutions. God's presence within creation, including among his people, is called immanence.

Jesus manifested God's name by Jesus himself being God's presence among men: he who has seen Jesus has seen the Father (Jn 14:9). God's immanence in the New Testament is ontological—it has to do with God "becoming" man in Jesus. The Incarnation affects all humanity. The Resurrection of Jesus means his body has become the new Temple, and through Jesus one day the whole of creation will become God's dwelling in a new way. Christ continues to make God known, so we can move beyond our limitations and he can draw us into communion with him.

(4) *Jesus' prayer for unity among his followers.* Christ prays for his future disciples to be one so that the world will recognize that the Father sent him (Jn 17:11, 21). In this way, Christian unity is tied to Christ's mission of restoring the world to the Father.

But what kind of unity does Jesus pray for? German biblical scholar and demythologizer Rudolf Bultmann held it was an invisible unity brought about by the proclamation of authentic word. Pope Benedict finds this claim astonishing. Jesus spoke of a unity that was also visible: people would recognize its extraordinary character and come to believe that God sent Jesus.

The unity for which Jesus prayed is based on faith in God and in Jesus as the one God sent. This faith is invisible but it has a visible aspect in that it unites believers in the visible body of the incarnate Word (Logos). This faith involves Jesus' disciples in the mission of faithfully proclaiming Jesus' message.

Apostolic succession keeps the content of faith concrete and authentic. The canon of Scripture and the rule of faith (*regula fidei*), which is a short summary (or creed) of the essential content of faith, are two other elements by which authentic proclamation is identified and maintained. These elements develop in order to realize the unity for which Jesus prays.

The mission of Jesus' disciples is to help people recognize and believe in God through Jesus Christ. "Recognition" and believing are not merely intellectual activities; they involve God's love transforming people's lives.

The Church's mission is universal—for the whole world. How is that universality reconciled with Jesus' high-priestly prayer, which he says he offers for those who believe and not for the whole world? John's Gospel uses the term "world" in two senses: (1) to refer to the whole of God's creation, which he loves, and (2) to the world of corruption and evil, which is hostile to God. Jesus' mission, which the Church continues, is to bring the world of corruption back into union with God, so that it is part of the good creation.

Jesus' high-priestly prayer of self-consecration and sacrifice establishes the Church, the community of disciples united through faith in Christ as the one sent by the Father and drawn into Jesus' mission to lead the world back to God.

Outline

I. The origin and meaning of the expression "high-priestly prayer"

A. Jesus' farewell discourses (Jn 14–16) follow the act of foot-washing and culminate in his "high-priestly prayer"

1. Lutheran theologian David Chytraeus coined the term "high-priestly prayer"

    2. Rupert of Deutz summarized the prayer's meaning: Jesus is the high priest who makes atonement and who is the sacrifice offered for us

II. The Jewish Feast of Atonement is the biblical background to Jesus' high-priestly prayer

  A. The Old Testament Feast of Atonement

    1. On the annual Day of Atonement the high priest offered sacrifices for his own sins, those of his priestly caste, and of all the people (Lev 16; 23:26–62)

    2. The feast restored Israel as God's people in the world

    3. Rabbinic theology of the Covenant

      a. The idea of the Covenant preceded the idea of creation

      b. Creation provided a "space" for the Covenant, the harmony of God and man

      c. The Feast of Atonement restored this harmony

  B. Jesus' prayer in John 17 is modeled on the ritual in Leviticus 16

    1. Jesus prayed for himself, for the Apostles, and for all believers—as the high priest made atonement for himself, the priesthood, and all the people

    2. Jesus is the high priest of the true Day of Atonement for the world

    3. The theology of John 17 corresponds to ideas in the Letter to the Hebrews and some of Saint Paul's ideas

  C. Jesus' high-priestly prayer is the culmination of the Day of Atonement

    1. The high-priestly prayer is not a Eucharistic Prayer but it is linked to the Eucharist

    2. Jesus transformed the ritual of the Day of Atonement into prayer to the Father

      a. Animal sacrifices have been replaced by "spiritual sacrifices"—worship shaped by the word and reason (Rom 12:1)

      b. The "word" of this sacrifice is the Word made flesh, who offered up his body and his blood

      c. Jesus transformed his cruel death into "word"—the expression of his self-giving love

      d. Jesus' self-giving sacrifice is tied to the Eucharist

  D. The Suffering Servant image, especially in Isaiah 53, prefigures Jesus' deepened, spiritual understanding of the priesthood

1. The Suffering Servant fulfills the ministry of high priest by "carrying" the sins of others and offering his life as a sin-offering
2. The Suffering Servant is both priest and victim
3. In John 10:11, 15, 17, 18, Jesus is linked to the Suffering Servant

E. Jesus' words and actions are outwardly discontinuous with the sacrificial system, yet he maintains a deep inner unity with the history of the Old Covenant

III. Four major themes of Jesus' prayer

A. "This is eternal life . . ."
   1. The theme of *zōē*-life as part of the "new liturgy of the Atonement"
   2. "Eternal life" is "true" or "real" life from God, which is not threatened by physical death
   3. Eternal life can be possessed now through "recognition" of (union of being with) God, who *is* life, and the one he has sent, Jesus Christ
   4. Plato took preliminary steps toward the biblical idea, but only Jesus fully and explicitly revealed it
   5. *Zōē*-life, as opposed to *bios*-life, or ordinary human life, is man's goal and death cannot take it away

B. "Sanctify them in truth . . ."
   1. Sanctification is linked to the idea of atonement and to the high priesthood
   2. Three sanctifications (or consecrations) in John
      a. Sanctification of the Apostles in the truth (Jn 17:17, 19)
      b. Jesus sanctifies himself
      c. The Father sanctifies the Son and sends him into the world (Jn 10:36)
   3. The biblical meaning of "to sanctify": "to make holy"
      a. In the full sense, holiness is attributable to God alone
      b. Holiness also refers to the quality of a person or a thing as being "set apart" from the rest of reality, from ordinary life
         1) Consecrated for sacrifice
         2) Priestly consecration, which designates a man for God and for conducting divine worship
   4. The meaning of the three sanctifications in John 17
      a. The Father's sending of the Son into the world and consecrating him (Jn 10:36)

        1) Jesus' consecration by the Father was identical to the Incarnation

        2) Jesus as the Holy One of God was united with the Father and as man existed for the mission to the world

    b. Jesus' self-consecration (Jn 17:19)

        1) Jesus consecrates, or dedicates himself, as high priest and as sacrifice

        2) Jesus is the sacrifice present in the Eucharist of all times

        3) Philo anticipated the idea of the Logos (Word) as high priest

        4) Jesus fulfilled the Day of Atonement since he is the Word made flesh for the life of the world (Jn 6:51)

    c. Sanctification of the disciples (Jn 17:19)

        1) John 17:19: the disciples are consecrated in the truth

        2) Old Testament background of priestly consecration of the Apostles

            a) In Exodus 29:1–9 Aaron's sons were consecrated priests when they vested in the sacred robes and were anointed

            b) The Day of Atonement ritual refers to Aaron completely bathing before investiture with his sacred robe (Lev 16:4)

            c) The disciples of Jesus at the Last Supper were consecrated in the bath of truth and were invested with the robe of truth; the truth is Christ himself

            d) Post-Temple Judaism reinterpreted sanctification and the cultic language to refer to obedience to God's will

            e) Jesus is the Torah in person, and priestly consecration comes through union with his will and his being

            f) The high-priestly prayer includes the institution of the Apostles' priesthood, the New Testament priesthood

C. "I have made your name known to them . . ."

    1. The revelation of God's name is a fundamental theme of the high-priestly prayer (Jn 17:6, 26)

        a. Jesus is the new Moses, revealing God's name

        b. The divine name was more than a word; it meant God entered into communion with Israel

        c. The divine name represented God's immanence—his presence among his people in their religious institutions

    2. Jesus manifests God's name by bringing a new, ontological mode of God's presence among men: he who has seen Jesus has seen the Father (Jn 14:9)

      a. The Incarnation affects all humanity

      b. Through Jesus' Resurrection, his body has become the new Temple

      c. Through Christ, creation will one day become God's dwelling in a new way

   3. "Name-Christology" of early Christianity: Christ in person is God's name

   4. Christ continues to make God known, so we can move beyond our limits and be drawn into communion with God

D. "That they may all be one . . ."

   1. Jesus prays for his future disciples' unity so that people will recognize that he was sent from the Father (Jn 17:11, 21)

   2. Why kind of unity did Jesus pray for?

      a. Bultmann: invisible unity among disciples affected by proclamation of the authentic tradition

      b. But the unity of which Jesus spoke is also visible; people would see its extraordinary character and believe in Jesus

   3. The nature and content of the unity for which Jesus prayed

      a. The element of faith

         1) The unity of the future Church rests on faith in God and in Jesus Christ as the one he sent

         2) This faith is invisible yet it has a visible aspect in that it unites individual believers in the visible body of the incarnate Logos (Word)

         3) Faith involves the mission of the proclamation of Jesus—his message, not man's

      b. Faith made concrete and its authenticity guaranteed in:

         1) Apostolic succession of the message and the messengers: continuation of the mission of the apostolic witnesses to Jesus and his message

         2) The canon of Scripture

         3) The rule of faith (*regula fidei*): a short summary of the essential content of the faith, the key to understanding the Scripture

   4. "Recognizing" and believing are not merely intellectual activities but involve being transformed by God's love

   5. Universality of the Church's mission is made visible: to the whole of creation

      a. John 3:16 and John 6:51 refer to Jesus' mission being for the world

    b. How to reconcile the universal mission with Jesus' statement that he prays for his disciples, not the world

       1) Two senses of "world" in John's Gospel

         a) Whole of God's good creation, which God loves

         b) The world of corruption and evil, alienated from God

       2) Jesus' mission is to bring the world of corruption back into union with God

  6. The high-priestly prayer of self-sanctification/sacrifice founded the Church, the community of disciples who are united through faith in Christ as the one sent by the Father and who are drawn into Jesus' mission to lead the world to God

Questions for Understanding

1. What is the Old Testament background to Jesus' high-priestly prayer in John 17 (pp. 77–78)?

2. What is "the object" of the Day of Atonement (p. 78)? How can one speak of this feast in relation to the whole of creation (p. 78)?

3. How does Jesus' high-priestly prayer follow the Day of Atonement ritual as presented in Leviticus 16 (pp. 78–79)?

4. Into what does Jesus transform the ritual of the Day of Atonement (pp. 80–81)? How does this transformation of worship relate to the Eucharist (p. 80)?

5. How is the vision of worship presented in John's Gospel related to the Suffering Servant Songs, especially Isaiah 53?

6. What are the four major themes of the high-priestly prayer selected by Benedict (p. 82)?

7. How is the meaning of "eternal life" in John different from what one might think (pp. 82–83)? How does one obtain it (p. 83)?

8. How is eternal life "a relational event" (p. 84)?

9. What does "sanctify" mean (p. 86)?

10. What are the two aspects of "sanctification" and how are they related to each other (p. 86)?

11. What does each of the three sanctifications mentioned in John 17 mean (pp. 87–90)?

12. How does Jesus present himself as the new Moses (p. 90)?

13. What does "God's name" mean (p. 91)? What does it mean for Christ to manifest God's name? What is the goal of the "manifestation" of God's name (p. 92)?

14. What is the final theme of Jesus' high-priestly prayer discussed by Benedict (p. 93)? How is Jesus' prayer for unity linked to his mission (p. 96)? How do we know from Jesus' prayer that he intends a visible unity for his disciples (p. 96)?

15. Identify three elements that Benedict says are fundamental to Christian unity (pp. 98–99).

16. How can Jesus' mission extend to the whole world if he prays only for his disciples and not for the whole world (pp. 100–101)?

17. In what sense does Jesus' prayer for unity among his disciples establish the Church (p. 101–2)?

Questions for Application

1. In what ways have I been "sanctified" by Jesus?

2. Have I come to "recognize" the true God and the one whom he has sent? What signs exist in my life to indicate that I have more than intellectual recognition?

3. How can the discussion of sanctity and sanctification assist me in sanctifying each moment of the day?

4. What are ways that I experience the gift of God's presence in my daily life?

5. How can we share in the mission of making known the name of the Father? Do I remember to pray for unity? Do I help promote unity?

Terms

Notes

CHAPTER FIVE

The Last Supper

Summary

The Last Supper accounts are more involved in conflicting hypotheses than even the eschatological discourse. Historical research cannot prove everything, but neither can it disprove the faith. In any event, it cannot provide the certainty of faith. However, historical research can show the historical plausibility of faith's basic convictions—including the events of the Last Supper, the Cross, and Resurrection of Jesus. Faith gives believers certainty, and it allows them serenely to consider various theories.

Four topics essential for the faith are considered: (1) the dating of the Last Supper and the related issue of whether it was a Passover meal; (2) the institution narratives; (3) the theology of the Last Supper tradition; and (4) the New Testament and the emergence of the Church's eucharistic tradition.

Regarding the dating of the Last Supper, the Synoptic Gospels (Matthew, Mark, and Luke) and the Gospel of John have different chronologies for the Last Supper and the death of Jesus. The Synoptics present the Last Supper as a Passover meal, which is eaten on the eve of the Passover feast. By that reckoning, Jesus died on the day of the Passover feast. The Last Supper would have taken place on Thursday evening. Jesus would have been arrested that night, and then tried and executed the next day, on Friday.

John's Gospel does not depict the Last Supper as a Passover meal—at least not in the conventional sense. The Last Supper was on the Thursday night before the eve of Passover, not on the eve of Passover as in the Synoptics. Jesus died on Friday, but it was the day before the Passover feast, not the day of the Passover feast. In John, Jesus died as the Passover lambs were slaughtered.

Scholars have tried to reconcile the Synoptics and John. Annie Jaubert's theory holds that Jesus followed a different liturgical calendar. According to that calendar, the eve of the Passover fell on Tuesday, while the calendar of the Jerusalem authorities put the eve of the Passover on Friday. The Synoptics reflect Jesus' celebration of the Passover meal on Tuesday night. John's Gospel follows the calendar of the Jerusalem authorities and puts Jesus' death on the eve of the Passover on Friday. Therefore, both the Synoptics and John are correct. Plus, there is additional time from Jesus' arrest on Tuesday until his crucifixion on Friday for his arrest and trial to occur.

Jaubert's thesis conflicts with the strong, early tradition of the Last Supper as having been on Thursday. Also, it is unlikely Jesus would have used an alternate calendar; he otherwise observes the Jewish feasts according to the Jerusalem calendar.

John P. Meier insists we must choose between the chronologies of the Synoptics and John. He favors John, whom he says is correct: Jesus died on the eve of Passover, as the lambs were slaughtered. The Passover-meal nature of the Last Supper comes from the fact that Jesus ate a final meal with his disciples and gave the meal a Passover meaning. Anticipating the Passover and his own death, Jesus offered himself as the Passover lamb and instituted the Eucharist as *his* Passover.

The four accounts of Jesus' institution of the Eucharist can be grouped according to the similarity of their wording: Mark/Matthew and Luke/1 Corinthians. Although the institution narratives are linked to the Church's later eucharistic celebrations, their liturgical use does not undercut their claims to historical authenticity. Their historical authenticity supports their liturgical use.

Some modern theologians reject the historical authenticity of the institution narratives. Their main argument is that there is an allegedly irreconcilable conflict between Jesus' message of God's forgiveness in the kingdom of God and the idea of Jesus' death as expiation for sins.

Yet there is no necessary unresolvable conflict between these two things. Some commentators argue that Jesus' message may have shifted as he met with opposition. This is plausible and there is evidence to support this idea. At the same time, Jesus' message seems from the beginning to have been shaped by the Cross. Thus, we have no reason to suppose Jesus could not have used the language of the Cross at the Last Supper. Only because Jesus spoke and acted as he did at the Last Supper would the Church from the beginning have celebrated the Eucharist.

The two strands of tradition regarding the Last Supper—Mark/Matthew and Paul/Luke—have their respective emphases. Mark/Matthew contain echoes of Exodus 24:8, in which the blood of the Covenant refers to the Israelites' sealing of the Covenant at Mount Sinai. Paul/Luke refer to Jeremiah 31:31, which speaks of the New Covenant. These texts reflect differences of emphasis and bring out one or the other elements in Jesus' words.

The name "Eucharist" developed from a Greek word meaning "thanksgiving". It derives from Jesus' act of giving thanks to God over the bread and wine of the Last Supper, which is itself a form of the Jewish *berakah*, or thanksgiving prayer. Jesus communicates and distributes himself—his whole self—to his disciples under the form of bread. The words spoken over the chalice recall the two texts cited above (Ex 24:8 and Jer 31:31), and Isaiah 53:12, from one of the Suffering Servant Songs. Jesus is the Suffering Servant who takes upon himself the sins of those who violated the Sinai Covenant. Through his obedience to the Father, Jesus establishes the New Covenant, and in the Eucharist gives himself in anticipation of his death and Resurrection.

There is controversy regarding what Jesus means when he speaks of his blood being poured out "for many". Some scholars argue that the phrase "for many" is a Semitic expression that refers to all human beings, while others insist it means the totality of Israel, not all men. "For many" is, on this view, linked to the Suffering Servant, who is said to take upon himself the sins of Israel. Only later did the Church extend "for many" to everyone.

Meanwhile, other scholars argue that while Jesus' death on the Cross is offered as a sacrifice "for all", what he gives "for many" at the Last Supper is the chalice. "For many" applies only to those who receive the sacrament, which is not "all".

However, Jesus uses "for many" nonrestrictively elsewhere, when he speaks of the Son of Man giving his life "for many" (Mk 10:45), where he clearly applies his words to his death on the Cross "for all". In other words, Jesus universalizes the mission of the Suffering Servant by linking it to his mission as the Son of Man. Under the Holy Spirit's guidance, the Church gradually came to see the universalistic aspect of Jesus' mission.

The institution narratives of the Last Supper constituted the founding of the Church. The Eucharist brings the Church into existence and bestows her unity and mission. This is because the Eucharist, as the gift of Jesus' body and blood, anticipates Jesus' death and Resurrection.

At the Last Supper Jesus instructs his disciples to repeat what he did. However, they are to repeat the action of the offering of Jesus' body and blood, not the Passover meal. The early Church's problems with a communal meal preceding the Eucharist (1 Cor 11:20–22, 34) eventually led to the separation of the Eucharist from the meal. The essential element of Jesus' thanksgiving prayer was retained—his thanks for the Father's hearing his prayer and gift of the Resurrection to come, which allowed Jesus to give his body and blood in the form of bread and wine as pledges of resurrection and eternal life.

Gradually, the early Church understood that the Eucharist involved a new form of worship. According to J. A. Jungmann, the Church celebrates the memorial of Jesus' sacrificial death, not per se the Last Supper itself.

The Eucharist is bound up with the Resurrection of Jesus. The early Church celebrated the Eucharist on Sunday, which became "the Lord's day" (Acts 20:6–11; 1 Cor 16:2; Rev 1:10; *Didachē* 14:1; Ignatius' Letter to the Magnesians 9:1).

By the early second century, the essential elements of Christian worship were in place. The liturgy of the Word, derived from the synagogue reading of Scripture and prayers, was combined with the celebration of the Eucharist.

Those who want the Eucharist to imitate only the Last Supper and not include the idea of the Resurrection of Jesus misunderstand. Such a "Eucharist" would not be the gift the Lord gave the Church. The Resurrection of Jesus is central to Christian worship. Jesus' prayer at the Last Supper anticipates his Resurrection and draws his followers into the process of transformation. The eucharistic gifts, we his disciples, and then the world through mission are being changed as we look forward to Christ's return (1 Cor 11:26).

Outline

I. Approach to the subject of the Last Supper accounts

   A. Different hypotheses make the real event seem impossible to access

   B. This book does not address every detailed question of text and history but focuses on becoming acquainted with the figure of Jesus

   C. Issues of historicity must still be addressed because faith does not rest on stories as mere symbols of meta-historical truths

      1. The problem of historical research, which can at most establish only high probability, not the certainty of faith

      2. Jeremias' effort to historically verify the words of Jesus (*ipsissima verba Iesu*) and its limits

   D. Expectations

      1. Historical research will not disprove the key words and events of the Last Supper

      2. Historical research by its nature cannot provide absolute certainty

      3. The issue, then, is whether the basic convictions of faith are historically plausible, not scientifically certain

      4. The historical reality of the Last Supper, the Cross, and Resurrection is important to the truth of Christianity

      5. Faith provides ultimate certainty and allows serene examination of various hypotheses

   E. Historical issues related to the Last Supper that are essential to the faith

      1. The dating of the Last Supper and whether it was a Passover meal

      2. The institution narratives of the Eucharist

      3. The theology of the Last Supper tradition

      4. The New Testament tradition and the emergence of the Church's Eucharist

II. The dating of the Last Supper

   A. Problem of dating due to the conflict between the Synoptics and John's Gospel

      1. Synoptics

         a. The Last Supper was Thursday night, on the eve of the Passover and therefore *was a Passover meal* (Mk 14:12, 17)

         b. Jesus' trial and crucifixion were on Friday, the *day of the Passover feast*, the day *after* the Passover lambs were killed

2. John's Gospel

    a. The Last Supper was on the Thursday night on the day *before* the eve of Passover, and therefore the Last Supper was *not a Passover meal*, at least in the conventional sense, following the accepted calendar

    b. Jesus' trial and crucifixion were on Friday, the Passover eve, and the day on which the Passover lambs were killed for the Passover meal to follow that evening—*the day before the Passover feast* (Jn 18:28)

B. Attempts to establish the chronology of events

  1. Increasingly scholars hold John's chronology to be more probable, but it remains a problem to deny the Passover character of the Last Supper

  2. Annie Jaubert's attempt to reconcile the two chronologies

    a. Jaubert's theory

      1) Jesus celebrated the Passover according to a different liturgical calendar than the Jerusalem authorities—that of Qumran

      2) Synoptics record Jesus' Passover meal according to the liturgical calendar Jesus followed; John's chronology follows that of the Jerusalem authorities, so both are correct

      3) The Last Supper occurred on Tuesday night, not Thursday

      4) Jesus' arrest and trial transpired over a couple of days, rather than in a single night and early morning

      5) The Jerusalem authorities tried to get Jesus condemned before Friday but his execution was delayed by Pilate's hesitations

    b. Benedict's reply

      1) The tradition of a Thursday Last Supper is firm while the Tuesday alternative is weak

      2) It seems unlikely that Jesus would have used an alternate calendar associated with Qumran, given that Jesus otherwise observed the Jewish festal calendar

  3. John P. Meier's analysis

    a. We must choose between the chronologies of the Synoptics and John, and the weight of the evidence favors John

    b. John is correct that Jesus died as the Passover lambs were being slaughtered

    c. Meier does not give a convincing answer as to why the Synoptics refer to a Passover—the Passover texts were added later

     d. Jesus knew he would die before the Passover meal, so he invited his disciples to a farewell dinner at which he gave himself as the true lamb and instituted *his Passover*

  4. Benedict's conclusion: Jesus' Last Supper anticipated the Cross and Resurrection in the eucharistic gifts and was regarded as *his Passover*

III. The institution of the Eucharist

  A. Four accounts of Jesus' institution of the Eucharist

    1. The Synoptics and Paul's First Corinthians

    2. Two basic models: Mark/Matthew and Paul/Luke

    3. Arguments regarding which is earlier, but both sets of text are early

    4. The liturgical use of the institution accounts does not undercut their historical authenticity; historical authenticity underwrites the liturgical use

  B. Modern theology's questioning of the institution of the Eucharist at the Last Supper

    1. The principal argument against the historical authenticity of the institution narrative accounts: an alleged insoluble contradiction between Jesus' message about God's forgiveness in the kingdom of God and the idea of his vicarious expiatory death

    2. Replies to the argument above

      a. There is no necessary contradiction between the message of God's forgiveness and expiation

      b. Some exegetes argue for a change in Jesus' teaching from its initial proclamation of God's kingdom to his identification of himself with the Suffering Servant

        1) It is plausible to posit a change in Jesus' approach as a result of the rejection of his initial message about the kingdom

        2) But the conclusion that he changed his approach is not something of which we can be certain

        3) Jesus' message seems to have been shaped from the outset by the Cross

        4) Thus, there is no reason to suppose he would not have used the language of the Cross to which the Last Supper accounts refer and which they presuppose

    3. Conclusion: Only because Jesus spoke and acted as depicted in the Last Supper narratives would the Church have from the beginning celebrated the breaking of the bread

IV. The theology of the words of institution

  A. Key differences of the two main strands of tradition regarding the Eucharist

    1. Mark/Matthew

      a. Words over the bread (Mk 14:22; Mt 26:26): "This is my body"

      b. Words over the chalice:

        1) Mark 14:24: "This is my blood of the Covenant, which is poured out for many"

        2) Matthew 26:28 adds: "for many, for the forgiveness of sins"

    2. Paul/Luke

      a. Words over the bread:

        1) Paul (1 Cor 11:24) and Luke (Lk 22:19), respectively, add "which is for you" and "which is given for you"

        2) Both include: "Do this in memory of me"

      b. Words over the chalice are similar in Paul and Luke, both mention the "cup" as the New Covenant in Jesus' blood:

        1) Paul adds the instruction "Do this, as often as you drink it, in remembrance of me" (1 Cor 11:25)

        2) Luke does not have the instruction to repeat but refers to Jesus' blood "which is poured out for you" (Lk 22:20)

    3. Background

      a. Mark/Matthew hear echoes of Exodus 24:8, the "blood of the covenant" referring to the sealing of the Covenant on Mount Sinai

      b. Paul/Luke allude to Jeremiah 31:31, which refers to the New Covenant

    4. The New Testament writers were strictly faithful in transmitting Jesus' words, and this is consistent with nuanced redaction that stresses one or the other element of Jesus' words

  B. Analysis of Jesus' words and actions in relation to the bread and the chalice

    1. The bread

      a. Jesus gives thanks, which indicates the *berakah*, Jewish thanksgiving prayer

        1) The Church offers with Jesus praise and thanksgiving through which God's earthly gift is given the new form of Jesus' body and blood, God's gift of himself in his Son's self-emptying love

        2) "Eucharist" (from *eucharistía*, meaning "thanksgiving") came to apply to the whole new act of worship given by Jesus

      b. Jesus "broke the bread"

        1) The act of the head of the family, an act of hospitality of sharing and welcome, given new depth when Jesus communicates and distributes himself in the form of bread

        2) The action comes to symbolize the whole mystery of the Eucharist: "the breaking of the bread"

      c. Words spoken over the bread: Jesus' body refers to the whole flesh-and-blood person, which includes his life freely given for others

  2. The chalice: words spoken over the chalice and three key Old Testament texts: Exodus 24:8; Jeremiah 31:31, and Isaiah 53:12

      a. Exodus 24:8: The sealing of the Covenant on Sinai

      b. Jeremiah 31:31: The New Covenant and the crisis of the Old Covenant

        1) New Covenant arises from the history of infidelity to the Old

        2) New Covenant fidelity is rooted in the obedience of the Son

        3) Reality of evil and of sin is confronted by God himself

      c. Isaiah 53:12: The Suffering Servant who bears the sins of "many"

        1) The Son acts as God toward man and as man toward God and atones for sin

        2) The vicarious sufferings of the Son, who has become a servant to bear sin and to obey

        3) The New Covenant in Jesus' blood—the total gift of himself, unconditionally faithful

        4) The new worship, established at the Last Supper, draws humanity into Christ's vicarious obedience

C. The debate about Jesus' blood being shed "for many" and "for you"

  1. The "for": Jesus' entire being expressed by "pro-existence"; his very being is a "being-for" others

  2. The meaning of "for many"

      a. Jeremiah's view: "for many" is a Semitism meaning "for all"

      b. Some more recent exegetes: "for many" cannot simply be equated with "all"

        1) Jesus uses it to refer to the totality of Israel

        2) "For all" was later extended when the Gospel was preached to the Gentiles

      c. Baumert and Seewann's view

    1) The death of Christ on the Cross is "for all"

    2) But at the Last Supper what is said to be poured out "for many" is the chalice, hence "for many" applies only to those who receive the sacrament, which is not "all"

  d. Benedict's view

    1) "For many" is used elsewhere in a nonrestrictive way that clearly applies to the Cross, not only to the Eucharist: "the Son of Man also came . . . to give his life as a ransom for many" (Mk 10:45)

    2) Jesus universalizes the mission of the Suffering Servant by linking it to the mission of the Son of Man

    3) Under the guidance of the Spirit, the early Church gradually came to see the universalistic aspect of Jesus' mission (cf. 1 Tim 2:6): the mission "for many" that Jesus understood as the mission "for all"

D. Jesus' words of institution and the founding of the Church

  1. Benedict approves Protestant theologian Ferdinand Kattenbusch's view that the words of institution constitute the founding of the Church

  2. The Church comes to be, and acquires her unity and mission, from the Eucharist

  3. The Church is derived from Jesus' death and Resurrection, which he anticipates in the gift of his body and blood at the Last Supper

V. From the Last Supper to the Sunday morning Eucharist

A. Jesus' instruction to repeat the Eucharist

  1. Paul and Luke explicitly indicate Jesus' instruction to repeat the eucharistic action; Mark and Matthew only imply it, but in either case the community of disciples was to repeat Jesus' action

  2. Which action?

    a. Not the Passover meal (if the Last Supper was a Passover meal)

    b. Jesus' new actions at the Last Supper, with their essential meaning in worship

B. Development of the Church's eucharistic worship

  1. Initially, the Eucharist was associated with a communal meal of bread and wine with the Eucharist at the end

  2. Later, problems with the meal aspect (1 Cor 11:20–22, 34) eventually led to a separation of the Lord's Supper from a regular meal

3. The elements for which Jesus gave thanks at the Last Supper point to the essential meaning of the Eucharist:

   a. the Father's hearing the prayer

   b. the gift of Jesus' Resurrection to come, which allowed Jesus to give his body and blood in the form of bread and wine as pledge of resurrection and eternal life

4. Gradual emergence of understanding in the early Church that the Eucharist involved a new form of worship

5. J. A. Jungmann's view: Church celebrates what the Lord instituted at the Last Supper—the memorial of his sacrificial death—not the Last Supper itself

C. The link between the Eucharist and the Resurrection of Jesus expressed in the Sunday celebration: on the "Lord's day" (Acts 20:6–11; 1 Cor 16:2; Rev 1:10; *Didachē* 14:1; Ignatius of Antioch, *Ad Magn.* 9:1)

1. The essential elements of Christian worship were in place by the early second century: the liturgy of the Word, derived from the synagogue, was joined to the celebration of the Eucharist

2. Imitating only the Last Supper and not including the Resurrection in eucharistic worship would not correspond to the Lord's gift

   a. The Resurrection is central to Christian worship

   b. Jesus' eucharistic prayer anticipates the Resurrection and draws us into the process of transformation—and draws us into the process of transformation, which moves from the Eucharistic gifts to us, to the world, until Jesus comes (1 Cor 11:26)

Questions for Understanding

1. Why does Benedict think that questions of the New Testament's historical authenticity are important (pp. 103–5)?

2. Although historical research is helpful, why can it not be the ultimate ground of the Christian faith (pp. 104–5)?

3. What is important for historical research to provide Christians regarding their faith (p. 105)?

4. What does well-grounded faith allow us to do when it comes to conflicting exegetical hypotheses (p. 105)?

5. How do the Synoptic Gospels differ from the Gospel of John when it comes to when the Last Supper and the crucifixion are said to have occurred (pp. 106–8)?

6. How does Annie Jaubert's theory attempt to reconcile the differences between the Synoptics and John's Gospel regarding the Last Supper and the crucifixion of Jesus (pp. 109–12)?

7. If the Last Supper was not a Passover meal in the usual sense, how does Benedict XVI think the early Church came to regard it as a Passover meal (pp. 112–15)?

8. Why do some theologians see a conflict between Jesus' teaching about the kingdom of God and his vicarious self-offering at the Last Supper and on the Cross (pp. 118–20)? What are some solutions to this alleged conflict (pp. 120–22)? What is Benedict's view (pp. 122–25)?

9. Why does Benedict think the evidence supports the authenticity of the Last Supper traditions (pp. 122–25)?

10. How does Benedict reconcile God's "unconditional forgiveness" with the truth of human evil and the idea of justice (pp. 133–34)?

11. In what way does God through Jesus establish a new and indestructible Covenant (p. 133)?

12. Summarize the different views of Jesus' words "for many" as he used them at the Last Supper (pp. 134–36). What is Benedict's view (pp. 136–37)?

13. How did Jesus change the "for Israel only" view of the Suffering Servant's mission (pp. 136–37)?

14. How is the Eucharist the foundation of the Church (p. 138)?

15. When Jesus told his disciples at the Last Supper to "Do this in remembrance of me", what did he intend them to repeat (p. 139)? For what did Jesus give thanks (pp. 140–41)? According to Josef A. Jungmann, what did Jesus institute at the Last Supper (pp. 141–42)?

16. How does the celebration of the Eucharist on the first day of the week indicate the Eucharist's link to the Resurrection (pp. 142–43)?

Questions for Application

1. Is your faith challenged or strengthened by historical research?

2. How do you respond when experts allege a conflict between things you believe as a matter of faith and what the experts claim that reason tells us?

3. The Passover feast was a celebration of Israel's bondage in Egypt. How is Jesus' offering of himself his "Passover" for us, and what difference does it make in your spiritual life?

4. How does the fact that Jesus instituted the Eucharist as a memorial of his death and Resurrection, as opposed to merely a community meal, affect the manner in which you participate in the Eucharist?

5. What does this chapter mean for your understanding of the idea that the Eucharist is "the source and summit of the Christian life", as the Second Vatican Council taught?

Terms

Baumert, Norbert, 135
Bonhoeffer, Dietrich, 133
Book of Jubilees, 109
day of preparation, 108
Didascalia Apostolorum, 111
Essenes, 111
etiology of worship, 117
factum est, 105
institution narrative, 115
ipsissima verba, 104

Jaubert, Annie, 109
Jeremias, Joachim, 104
Jungmann, Josef Andreas, 141
Kattenbusch, Ferdinand, 138
Lohfink, Gerhard, 120
Peterson, Erik, 121
praetorium, 108
Seewann, Maria-Irma, 135

Notes

CHAPTER SIX

Gethsemane

Summary

Following the Last Supper the Lord leads his disciples to the Mount of Olives, to a place called Gethsemane (meaning "oil press"). Along the way, the worship of the Upper Room spills out into the night as the group continues to chant hymns, perhaps the Hallel Psalms traditionally sung at Passover (Ps 113–18 and 136). These express not only words of praise and thanksgiving, but as Benedict notes, they provide a glimpse of the paschal mystery coming to fulfillment in Jesus, who is the "rejected stone" destined to become the honored "cornerstone" of a new Temple (see Ps 118:22).

In praying the Psalms, Christ prays in union with Israel, celebrating the liberation of his people from Egypt, yet he also looks ahead to a new Passover deliverance that will embrace the world. Three prophecies about this paschal event are uttered in the course of the journey: one that foresees a Messianic "shepherd" struck down in death while his "sheep" are scattered (Zech 13:7; Mt 26:31); another that promises Jesus will be "raised up" and "go before" his disciples to Galilee (Mk 14:28); and a third regarding Peter's threefold denial of the Master (Mt 26:33–35).

Psalmody and prophecy give way to private prayer when the group reaches Gethsemane. Pope Benedict sees the whole drama of our redemption made present in the struggle that follows. On the one hand, the humanity of Jesus trembles with the primordial fear of created nature in the face of death. On the other, the agony of the Son is even more extreme because he perceives the full power of evil that is unleashed upon him. Audible in the prayer of Jesus is a confrontation between his "natural will", which desires to be saved from the horrors to come, and his "filial will" (p. 156), which abandons itself to the Father's plan (Mt 26:39; Mk 14:36; cf. Jn 12:27–28).

To shed light on this mystery of the two wills, Benedict turns to the Ecumenical Councils of the Church. The Council of Chalcedon (A.D. 430), in particular, provides an important key to the Gethsemane episode. By insisting that Jesus was both fully God and fully man, and that his humanity must not be confused with his divinity, the Council laid the groundwork for seeing that Jesus must possess a human will in addition to his divine will. At first glance, this could seem to imply that Jesus had a dual or schizophrenic personality. But such is not the case. In the person of Jesus, the human will is so perfectly attuned to the divine will that the two operate in unison. And since doing God's will is the purpose for which the human will was made, one can say with Maximus the Confessor that the human will of Jesus experiences its fulfillment—rather than its annihilation—when it acts in conformity with God's will. Moreover, man's true greatness is restored by this "working together" of wills in Christ; it indicates that human nature's resistance to God is transformed through the sacrificial obedience of the Son.

Finally, Benedict considers an allusion to Jesus' agony in the Letter to the Hebrews. He holds that Hebrews 5:7, which looks back on the sufferings and supplications of Christ, represents a tradition concerning the event that is distinct from what is found in the Gospels. One reason for this assessment is that it extends beyond Gethsemane to encompass the crucifixion, as indicated by its reference to the "loud cries" that Jesus uttered on the Cross (Mt 27:46, 50; Mk 15:34, 37). The point in Hebrews is that the entire Passion of Christ is an action of prayer—a plea to the Father for deliverance from death. Theologically, this is an exercise of the high priesthood of Jesus, who offers himself in sacrifice to the Father's will. Moreover, the remark that Jesus' prayer "was heard" and ultimately granted points to the Resurrection. It is not that Christ was spared the bitter experience of death, but that he was rescued from death in a permanent way by his rising from the grave, never to die again. Indeed, his death was a conquest of death itself and thus a source of salvation and life for all who obey him (cf. Heb 5:8–10).

Outline

I. On the way to the Mount of Olives

A. Jesus and the Hallel Psalms sung at Passover (Ps 113–18, 136)

B. Christian reading of the Psalms takes place in communion with Christ, the new David, much as Israel prayed in solidarity with David of old

C. Gethsemane: site of ancient oil press; site of the modern Church of Jesus' Agony; site of Jesus' night of final loneliness and anguish

D. Jesus utters three prophecies

1. The "shepherd" will be struck down, the "sheep" scattered (Mt 26:31)

2. Jesus will be raised, his sheep regathered (Mk 14:28)

3. Peter will deny Jesus three times (Mt 26:34)

II. The prayer of Jesus

A. Gethsemane episode in the New Testament

1. Synoptic Gospels (Mt 26:36–46; Mk 14:32–42; Lk 22:39–46)
2. John's Gospel (Jn 12:27–28)
3. Letter to the Hebrews (Heb 5:7–10)

B. Summons to vigilance ("remain here, and watch", Mk 14:34)

1. Drowsiness of disciples makes them vulnerable to the Evil One
2. Kneeling posture of Jesus makes him the model of Christian martyrs

C. Gethsemane prayer ("not what I will, but what you will", Mk 14:36)

1. Human nature trembles before death; the Son trembles before sin and evil
2. The mystery of Jesus' two wills, "natural" (human) and "filial" (divine)
3. Acceptance of the "chalice" as the glorification of God (see Jn 12:28)

III. **Jesus' will and the Father's will**

A. Council of Chalcedon (A.D. 451): the Son of God is one "person" with two "natures"

B. Debate after Chalcedon: What is the status of Christ's human nature?

1. Heresy of monothelitism denied that Jesus possessed a true human will
2. Maximus the Confessor affirmed that Jesus possessed a true human will, as witnessed in the Gethsemane episode, and that he aligned his human and divine wills with the Father's will

C. Jesus' prayer of consent draws human opposition to God back into union with God

D. Jesus, using the intimate language of children, prays to "Abba, Father" (Mk 14:36)

IV. **Jesus' prayer in the Letter to the Hebrews**

A. Hebrews 5:7 covers the whole Passion of Jesus up to his "loud cries" on the Cross

B. Jesus' cries and pleas are an exercise of his high priesthood

1. His prayers and supplications are "offered" like a sacrifice (Heb 5:7)
2. Through suffering he was "made perfect" as a consecrated priest (Heb 5:9)

C. Jesus' prayer to be saved from death granted through his Resurrection

D. Jesus' deliverance from death as conquest of death "for others"

Questions for Understanding

1. How does Pope Benedict see Jesus in relation to David (pp. 146–47)? How does this transform a Christian reading and praying of the Psalms (pp. 146–47)?

2. Benedict finds it significant that the Gospel of John locates the agony, the crucifixion, and the Resurrection of Jesus in a "garden" (Jn 18:1; 19:41). He calls this an unmistakable reference to what story in the Old Testament (pp. 149–50)? Why is this significant?

3. Luke alone notes that Jesus was kneeling as he prayed in Gethsemane. What is the message conveyed by this (p. 154)? How does Benedict support this understanding from the Acts of the Apostles (p. 154)?

4. Jesus speaks of "my will" and "thy will" in his Gethsemane prayer. Explain the former in light of Benedict's reflection, and identify who is addressed by the latter (see pp. 161–62).

5. The Letter to the Hebrews describes the Passion of Jesus in priestly and sacrificial terms. What two expressions (one in Heb 5:7 and the other in 5:9) lead Benedict to view the Gethsemane episode in this way (p. 164)?

Questions for Application

1. At several points during the Passion we see Jesus invoking the Psalms. Do you think it significant that Jesus relied on this book during the darkest moments of his life? Why? How might the Psalms be said to sustain the troubled soul?

2. When Jesus addressed his disciples in Gethsemane, he urged them to "watch" (Mk 14:34). In view of Benedict's commentary on this (pp. 152–53), what in today's world induces a drowsiness of the soul?

3. Have you ever prayed "not my will but thine" in difficult circumstances? Did you find that your surrender to God's will was worth the effort to renounce your own desires? Did you sense that God supplied the strength to follow through on your resolution? What good resulted from it?

4. Benedict offers the reflection that "my own sin was present in that terrifying chalice" offered to Jesus in Gethsemane (p. 156). Have you ever pictured Jesus agonizing at the prospect of shouldering the burden for your personal sins? Beyond stirring up pious sentiments, does it increase your desire to repent and to change the way you live?

5. Jesus addressed the Father using the Aramaic term "Abba". It bespeaks a relationship of tender familiarity such as children often have with their human fathers. How is your view of prayer and of your relationship with God affected by this background information? Do you think it encourages us to pray to our heavenly Father with confidence? Humility? Affection?

Terms

Council of Chalcedon, 157

Hallel Psalms, 145

Kroll, Gerhard, 148

Leo the Great, 158

Maximus the Confessor, 160

monophysitism, 159

monothelitism, 159

Nestorianism, 159

Schönborn, Christoph, 161

Stöger, Alois, 154

Vanhoye, Albert, 164

via dolorosa, 163

(von) Harnack, Adolf, 165

Notes

CHAPTER SEVEN

The Trial of Jesus

Summary

The Jerusalem authorities had little interest in Jesus before Palm Sunday. However, once he rode into the city and was hailed as Messiah, followed by his dramatic cleansing of the Temple, the preacher from Nazareth could no longer be ignored. Action had to be taken lest the volatile Passover crowds got out of hand.

Even before this, however, the Sanhedrin had met to discuss the popularity of Jesus after the raising of Lazarus. John's Gospel informs us of the gathering where the decision to eliminate Jesus initially took shape (see Jn 11:47–53). This was primarily the doing of the high priest, Caiaphas, who portrayed Jesus as a national threat to the Jewish people and their sanctuary. Unaware of the full import of his words, the high priest advised that "one man should die for the people" (Jn 11:50). This statement, intended to be pragmatic, was in reality prophetic—made possible by the charism of his office as Israel's chief religious authority. Caiaphas had unwittingly proclaimed the truth that Jesus was destined to die in a vicarious way "for" others. It was an advance glimpse of Christ assuming the role of the Suffering Servant described in Isaiah 53.

The prophecy of Caiaphas approached its fulfillment when authorities arrested Jesus and brought him before a late-night gathering of the Sanhedrin. There, in the palace of the high priest, he was accused of opposing the Temple and of assuming the role of a divine Messiah. Benedict suggests that the court interpreted this as a double strike at the heart of Judaism: its life of sacred worship and its faith in only one God (pp. 176–77). Beyond this, the anger of Caiaphas boiled over when Jesus directly affirmed his Messiahship and proceeded to qualify current Messianic expectations by referencing Psalm 110:1 and Daniel 7:13, passages that describe his kingly mission in heavenly terms rather than political or military terms (see Mk 14:61–62). This the Sanhedrin found intolerable: Jesus had claimed for himself a nearness to God that was perceived as blasphemy, as a crime worthy of death. Thereafter, Jesus was mocked and abused by his judges, again confirming his identity as the Suffering Servant of Isaiah.

In the third stage of the trial, Jesus was presented as a criminal to the governor, Pontius Pilate, who alone had the authority to carry out a death sentence in Roman

Palestine. The Sanhedrin stressed that Jesus had declared himself a king. The charge was calculated to resonate with Pilate, who would then be forced to deal with Christ as a political troublemaker challenging the authority of Caesar. Still, despite the accusations of the Temple leadership and the clamoring of the crowd for his death, Pilate could find no wrongdoing in Jesus worthy of condemnation.

This is brought out clearly in John's Gospel in the conversation between Jesus and Pilate (Jn 18:33–38). Here Jesus elucidates the unique nature of his kingship as something "not of this world" (Jn 18:36). Far from being a political entity supported by military strength, his kingdom is one that rests on a foundation of "truth" (Jn 18:37); it is based upon the priority of God's will in all things and an understanding of reality from God's perspective. Pilate had little interest in such talk and dismissed the issue with his sceptical comment "What is truth?" (Jn 18:38). It was clear to the governor that the so-called King of the Jews was not a genuine threat to his interests. Whatever Jesus meant by his otherworldly kingship, it seemed to be both peaceful (no one was fighting for it) and powerless (it was not competing for Caesar's earthly dominion).

Nevertheless, as Benedict points out, Pilate came to betray the truth by sentencing Jesus to die. He caved under the pressure of the Sanhedrin, who threatened the governor's career with the words "If you release this man, you are not Caesar's friend" (Jn 19:12). Unwilling to risk his position, Pilate brushed the truth of the matter aside in favor of the more practical concept of law, which could be used to maintain order and discourage any further disturbances. Peace, in other words, was valued above justice. As a result, the innocent Jesus was led off to be brutally scourged and mockingly crowned as one more victim of the inhumanity of worldly power.

Outline

I. Preliminary discussion in the Sanhedrin

A. Authorities unconcerned about Jesus until Palm Sunday and the raising of Lazarus

B. Early session of the Sanhedrin in John's Gospel (Jn 11:47–53)

1. Fear that the Romans will destroy the Temple and nation of Israel (Jn 11:48)

2. Religion and politics interwoven in the outlook of the Jewish leadership

3. Jesus' nonpolitical Messianic kingdom separates religion and politics

4. Caiaphas utters prophecy: "one man should die for the people" (Jn 11:50)

5. The mystery of vicarious atonement—Jesus will die "for" salvation of others

6. The "children of God" gathered and unified in the Church (Jn 11:52)

II. Jesus before the Sanhedrin

A. Jesus is led by night to the high priest's palace for cross-examination

B. Charges circulating against Jesus

　1. He spoke blasphemous words against the Temple

　2. He made a blasphemous claim to divine Messiahship

C. Caiaphas' question and Jesus' answer

　1. Jesus accepts the Messianic title ("I am", Mk 14:62)

　2. Jesus defines his Messianic identity in scriptural terms (Ps 110:1; Dan 7:13)

　3. Caiaphas tears his robes in outrage (Mk 14:63)

D. Jesus, mocked and abused, fulfills the destiny of Isaiah's Suffering Servant

E. Peter denies Jesus three times in the palace forecourt (Mk 14:66–72)

III. Jesus before Pilate

A. The Sanhedrin needs Pontius Pilate to sentence and execute Jesus

B. The claim of royal Messiahship is presented as a political crime against Rome

C. Who were Jesus' accusers?

　1. John's Gospel singles out "the Jews", meaning the Temple aristocracy

　2. Mark's Gospel adds the amnesty "crowd", meaning the followers of Barabbas

　3. Matthew's Gospel mentions "all the people" for whom Jesus sheds his blood

D. The figure of Pontius Pilate

　1. He could be brutal, but otherwise decisive and practical-minded

　2. He found in Jesus no serious threat to Roman order

E. Jesus' confession before Pilate

　1. His kingship is "not of this world" (Jn 18:36)

　2. His kingship is founded on "truth" rather than worldly power (Jn 18:37)

F. Answers to Pilate's sceptical remark "What is truth?" (Jn 18:38)

　1. Truth is conformity between intellect and reality

　2. Truth is ultimately God himself and his creative intellect

　3. Truth is giving priority to God and his will

　4. Truth includes—but extends beyond—the functional facts of science

5. Truth becomes recognizable when God becomes recognizable in Jesus Christ

G. The kingdom of God as the new kingship of truth proclaimed by Jesus

H. Pilate superstitious and fearful: Is condemning Jesus opposing divine power?

I. Pilate is threatened: "If you release this man, you are not Caesar's friend" (Jn 19:12)

J. Interlude in three acts

1. Candidates for Passover amnesty—Jesus or Barabbas

2. Scourging of Jesus—barbaric prelude to execution

3. Crowning with thorns and mock royal homage

K. "Ecce Homo": "Here is the man!" (Jn 19:5)

1. Suffering of the world's inhumanity displayed in the tortured figure of Jesus

2. God, still present in Jesus, is on the side of those who suffer

L. "Here is your King!" (Jn 19:14); death sentence pronounced upon Jesus

1. Pilate turns his back on justice

2. Pragmatism of law and order prevails over truth

Questions for Understanding

1. Benedict makes the point that Jesus detached religion from politics, two dimensions of life once inseparable in biblical Judaism. What event, according to the Pope, made this separation possible (pp. 170–71)? What does this say about "the new manner of God's dominion in the world" (p. 171)?

2. According to John's Gospel, Caiaphas prophesied that Jesus must die lest the Jewish nation perish at the hands of the Romans (Jn 11:50). What accounts for his ability to speak as a prophet in spite of his unworthy intentions (pp. 171–72)? What is the deeper meaning of his words?

3. John's Gospel indicates that "the Jews" accused Jesus before Pontius Pilate. Who, according to Benedict, is designated by this expression (p. 185)? Likewise, Mark's Gospel speaks of a mob-like "crowd" that demanded the crucifixion of Jesus. What group, according to the Pope, formed the main presence in this crowd (pp. 185–86)?

4. Matthew's Gospel quotes the crowd that was clamoring for Jesus' death as saying, "His blood be on us and on our children!" (Mt 27:25). What two levels of meaning does Benedict discern in these words (pp. 186–88)?

5. When Pilate listened to Jesus describe the nature of his kingship, his scepticism took the form of a question: "What is truth?" (Jn 18:38). According to Pope Benedict, how did Saint Thomas Aquinas answer this important question (p. 192)? How does Benedict answer it (p. 194)?

6. In what way did Pilate's "career goals" overcome his fear regarding Jesus' identity (pp. 195–96)? How does Benedict think Pilate's decision to execute Jesus shows how regard for a certain kind of "peace" trumped justice (pp. 200–201)?

Questions for Application

1. Benedict is obviously concerned to identify correctly those responsible for the condemnation of Jesus. What misinterpretation do you think he wants us to avoid? Do you, or someone you know, harbor anti-Jewish sentiments based on the story of the Passion? How does the Pope's reading of the Gospels give you a clearer perspective on this issue?

2. In reflecting on the conversation between Jesus and Pilate, Benedict poses an important question to contemporary society: "[W]hat happens when truth counts for nothing? What kind of justice is then possible?" (p. 191). How would you answer these questions, knowing what you do about some of the policies imposed by modern governments? What is the danger of excluding the question of truth from civic life and relegating it to the sphere of personal and private life?

3. Benedict states that Jesus' followers were hiding in fear as his trial unfolded. What are some ways that modern Christians have failed to come forth and make their voice heard in the public arena? What injustices are allowed to flourish because the truth is kept silent by those who know better?

4. Benedict sees both the suffering of humanity as well as the cruelty of earthly power in the scourged figure of Jesus. Few of us have ever wounded another in such a violent, physical way. But how many times have we injured others, even those we love most, by our gossip, our selfishness, our cutting comments, or our thoughtlessness? How does this image of Jesus, made to suffer at the hands of another, help you to think differently about other people? What do you think Benedict means when he says, "God is on the side of those who suffer" (p. 200)?

Terms

Brown, Raymond E., 184
Caiaphas, 167
Collins, Francis S., 193
Dodd, Charles H., 184
Mishna, 175
ochlos, 185

Pax Romana, 189
Sanhedrin, 167
scapegoat, 199
Schürmann, Heinz, 174
vicarious atonement, 172
vox populi, 186

Notes

CHAPTER EIGHT

Crucifixion and Burial of Jesus

Summary

Benedict opens the chapter by considering the numerous Old Testament references in the Passion narratives. In these accounts the words of Scripture and the events of history are tightly interwoven and mutually illuminating. Scripture unlocks the meaning of the event, just as the event provides a fresh understanding of Scripture. It took time for the infant Church to come to this understanding. The Pope describes it as a "process of searching and maturing" (p. 203), and he sees it unfolding on the road to Emmaus, where two disciples, who found the crucifixion inexplicable, journey with the Lord until they arrive at enlightenment through the Scriptures (Lk 24:13–35).

Benedict's meditation on the crucifixion begins with Jesus' prayer "Father, forgive them; for they know not what they do" (Lk 23:34). These words show us, not a man who is hateful or vengeful, but one who seeks mercy even for those who do him harm. The motive for Christ's supplication is the spiritual incomprehension of his opponents, which is something that can lead to conversion, such as happened with Saint Paul (1 Tim 1:13). Among these opponents are those who mock the Lord in his time of humiliation. The passers-by challenge Jesus to save himself, much as the devil had done to tempt him in the wilderness, and the Sanhedrin takes up words from Wisdom 2:18 to question his claim to the Son of God (Mt 27:43). One of the two criminals who are crucified beside Jesus derides him as well. The other, however, comes to faith in the final hour and is promised a place in Paradise (see Lk 23:40–43).

On the Cross Jesus quotes the first line of Psalm 22: "My God, my God, why have you forsaken me?" (Ps 22:1). Not only does this psalm permeate the whole of the Passion story, but according to Benedict, the whole of the psalm is implicitly present in its opening words. Jesus unites himself with the painful experience of Israel crying out to a God who seems hidden and absent. But the storyline of the psalm moves from tribulation to trust and the psalmist (and thus Jesus) becomes confident of God's deliverance. Jesus' cry of abandonment is not a bout with despair but one that includes the certainty of divine salvation. Psalm 22 points beyond the Passion to envision the gathering of the nations into the assembly of God's people and the poor having their fill—events that Christian interpretation links with the founding of the Church and the celebration of the Eucharist. Psalm 22, then, anticipates the salvation of Jesus (the Resurrection) and many others besides (the conversion of the Gentiles).

Other events follow that continue to fulfill the Scriptures. Casting lots for Jesus' garments recalls Psalm 22:18 (Jn 19:24), and the seamless tunic that Jesus wore (Jn 19:23) may be an allusion to his priestly dignity, for the Jewish historian Josephus describes the garment of Israel's high priest in similar terms. Likewise, when the soldiers offer Jesus a drink of vinegar or sour wine (Jn 19:28–30), echoes can be heard of the passion of the just man in Psalm 69, who laments: "for my thirst they gave me vinegar to drink" (Ps 69:21). Benedict also detects an allusion to Isaiah's parable of the vineyard, in which the covenant people, despite Yahweh's loving care, produced only wild and sour grapes (Is 5:4).

Though all the Gospels mention the presence of women at the foot of the Cross, only John's Gospel features the touching account of Jesus giving his Mother into the care of the beloved disciple (Jn 19:25–27). On a historical level, this reveals the genuinely human concern of a son for the well-being of his mother in his absence. Jesus arranges for his closest disciple to be his Mother's caretaker and protector. On another level, Mary and John are not simply historical figures; they represent the Church and all disciples who are loved by Jesus. Every disciple of Christ is gifted with a spiritual mother in Mary and in the Church, and both Mary and the Church are entrusted with the spiritual care of every follower of Christ. This deeper significance is suggested, in part, by Jesus addressing his Mother as "woman"—an allusion to her role as the new Eve (see Gen 2:23), who belongs to Jesus Christ, the new Adam.

What follows is the account of Jesus dying on the Cross. This is both a "cosmic" and a "liturgical" event. Its cosmic dimension is indicated by the darkening of the sun above and the quaking of the earth below. Its liturgical dimension is revealed by the tearing of the Temple veil, which indicates that the ancient rites and sacrifices must now pass away as the Cross replaces all other acts of worship. This new worship is signified by the blood and water that issue from the Lord's crucified body (Jn 19:34). The Fathers of the Church saw in these elements the two fundamental sacraments of the Christian religion: Baptism and the Eucharist. Also in this moment, the church of the Gentiles is born as a Roman centurion comes to believe that the crucified Jesus is, in fact, "the Son of God" (Mk 15:39).

The events of Good Friday end with two members of the Jewish ruling class preparing Jesus' body for burial (Jn 19:38–42). The linen cloths and the hundred pounds of spices are quite extravagant, leading Benedict to suggest that Christ is given, not an ordinary burial, but a "royal burial" suited to a king.

From the perspective of salvation history, the Cross succeeds where the sacrificial cult of the Temple failed, for it achieves the true and definitive removal of sins. The Pope's reflections are grounded partly in Romans 3:25 and partly in Hebrews 10:1–10 (with its quotation from Ps 40:6–7). From the latter text especially, Benedict explains that obedience to the Father's will is the true form of worship the world has been waiting for, the one form of sacrifice that truly glorifies God. The incarnate obedience of Jesus, reaching its fullest extent on the Cross, is the new sacrifice that takes away our sin and renders to God the obedience to this word that is due from the human family. This is the true essence of atonement and reconciliation with God. Through the sacraments, we can now be taken up into the body of Christ and become beneficiaries of his obedience and sharers in the salvation that he died to give us.

Outline

I. **Word and event in the Passion narrative**

    A. Multiple references to the Old Testament in the Passion accounts

        1. Scripture and events of the Passion interwoven throughout

        2. Meaning of both "word" and "event" discovered on road to Emmaus (Lk 24:13–35)

        3. Psalm 22: The psalmist's cry of anguish transforms into a profession of trust; the Church sees supplicant's prayer answered in the Resurrection (v. 25), the afflicted being satisfied with the Eucharist (v. 26), and universal salvation realized in the conversion of the Gentiles (v. 27)

        4. Isaiah 53: The prophet speaks as an evangelist

    B. Jesus on the Cross

        1. Jesus' first words, "Father, forgive them, for they know not what they do" (Lk 23:34)

            a. Jesus knows no hatred, makes no call for revenge

            b. Theme of "not knowing" echoed in Peter's Pentecost sermon (Acts 3:17), reappears in Saint Paul's autobiographical reflections (1 Tim 1:13) and is further exampled in the story of the wise men (Mt 2:4–6)

            c. Knowledge can blind us to the Truth; ignorance can open a door to conversion

        2. Jesus is mocked

            a. Passers-by challenge Jesus: "save yourself" (Mk 15:30). They are unaware that the era of the old Temple is giving way before the crucified Jesus, God's new Temple, who reconciles us with God and opens access to him

            b. Members of the Sanhedrin mock his claim to be "the Son of God", echoing words from the Book of Wisdom (Wis 2:10–20). Jesus' deliverance will come, not by dismounting the Cross, but in the Resurrection

    c. Two robbers crucified with Jesus—one joins in the mockery, the other grasps the mystery of Christ and his "kingly power" (Lk 23:42). He is offered fellowship with God in "Paradise" (Lk 23:43). Good thief is an image of hope in God's mercy offered to the very end

3. Cry of abandonment: "My God, my God, why have you forsaken me?" (Mt 27:46)

    a. Opening verse of Psalm 22, but misunderstood as a call to Elijah

    b. Jesus bears the anguish of all who suffer from God's silence and hiddenness and brings it as a prayer before God

    c. The whole of Psalm 22 is essentially present when Jesus utters its opening line, including the certainty that God will answer his prayer (in the Resurrection)

    d. Church Fathers: Jesus prays, not as an individual only, but also as a corporate personality, i.e., he prays both as head (the one who incorporates us into himself) and as body (our voices, anguish, and hope are present in his prayer)

4. Casting lots for Jesus' garments

    a. Fulfillment of Scripture (Ps 22:18 quoted in Jn 19:24)

    b. Jesus' seamless tunic: an allusion to his high-priestly dignity

    c. Church Fathers: seamless tunic an image of Church's indivisible unity

5. Jesus' words "I thirst" (Jn 19:28)

    a. Soldiers offer Jesus sour wine (or vinegar) to quench his thirst

    b. Brings to mind Psalm 69, in which the suffering psalmist is given "vinegar to drink" by his enemies (v. 21), as well as Isaiah's song of the vineyard, in which God laments that Israel produced only "wild grapes" (Is 5:2)

    c. Jesus addresses also the Church with his desires for wine (justice and love) rather than vinegar (human self-concern)

6. Women at the foot of the Cross—the Mother of Jesus

    a. Zechariah's prophecy, "they shall look on him whom they have pierced" (Zech 12:10), fulfilled in the faithful women (Jn 19:37)

    b. Jesus entrusts the beloved disciple to his Mother: "Woman, behold your son!" (Jn 19:26); likewise, his Mother is given into the care of the beloved disciple: "Behold your mother!" (Jn 19:27)

        1) Mary addressed as "Woman" recalls the creation of Adam's companion, also called "Woman" (Gen 2:23)

2) She belongs to Jesus, the new Adam, in whom humanity begins afresh

3) Human gesture with a deeper significance: the Woman is Mary herself, but also an image of the Church as bride and mother; the beloved disciple is a type of the true disciple entrusted with Mary and the Church

7. Jesus dies on the Cross

a. Luke gives Jesus' words: "Father, into your hands I commit my spirit" (Lk 23:46), a reference to Psalm 31:5

b. John gives Jesus' words: "It is finished!" (Jn 19:30)

1) A possible indication that Jesus' death is an act of priestly consecration (as in Heb 5:9)

2) It shows the Cross to be an act of worship that surpasses all others

c. The Church of the Gentiles is born through the confession of the Roman centurion: "Truly, this man was the Son of God" (Mk 15:39)

d. Jesus is the true Paschal Lamb, whose bones are not broken (Ex 12:46; Jn 19:33); he is the afflicted just man whose bones are unbroken (Ps 34:19–20)

e. Blood and water from the pierced heart of Jesus

1) These indicate the dual importance of Jesus' baptism and crucifixion, according to the Church Fathers

2) These also symbolize the two fundamental sacraments, Eucharist and Baptism, as well as the birth of the Church from the side of the new Adam

C. Jesus' burial

1. Burial accounts reveal "the other Israel"

a. Those who await the fulfillment of God's promises and recognize the kingdom of God making its entrance into the world through Jesus

b. Secret disciples: certain members of the educated ruling class in Israel (Joseph of Arimathea, Nicodemus)

2. The body is wrapped in linen cloths according to normal Jewish burial customs (Jn 19:40); however, it is also anointed with a hundred pounds of myrrh and aloes, suggesting a "royal burial" fit for a king

3. Several women prepare spices to conclude burial rites on Easter morning (Lk 23:56) only to discover that God preserved Jesus from death in a definitive way

II. Jesus' death as reconciliation (atonement) and salvation

A. The Cross of Christ supersedes the sacrifices of the Temple

    1. Critique of Temple worship in the Prophets and Psalms

        a. Ultimately, God was not glorified by the blood of animals, which was powerless to wipe away sins

        b. Atonement was finally achieved through the Lamb of God

    2. Much dispute in the early Church over the continuing validity of the Mosaic Law, as seen especially in Saint Paul's letters; however, there was no dispute that the cultic sacrifices of the Temple had ceased to be relevant for Christians

B. The Cross of Christ as the new worship

    1. Saint Paul compares Jesus with the covering of the Ark of the Covenant, the place where expiation of sin takes place and reconciliation between God and man is accomplished (Rom 3:25)

    2. Some object to the notion that God demands infinite atonement from man; yet the Christian concept of atonement holds that God took it upon himself to restore justice to the world through love by confronting the reality of sin and drinking its horrors down to the dregs

C. Atonement in the Letter to the Hebrews (Heb 10:1–7)

    1. Quotation from the Greek version of Psalm 40:6–8 read as a dialogue between the Son and the Father; the new worship established through the Incarnation, in particular the Son's obedience to God's word replaces the Temple sacrifices

    2. Several books of the Old Testament are aware that obedience to the word of God is true worship

        a. At the same time, they are also aware that human obedience is inconsistent and therefore inadequate to achieve atonement

        b. This gives rise to the longing that God will receive a gift from us that is more than we can give

    3. The perfect obedience of the incarnate Word fulfills this longing; his obedience as a man is the new sacrifice that wipes away our disobedience, for the Son gives to God the worship that we could not

D. Existential dimension of the Cross

    1. Saint Paul relates our sacrifice to Christ's with the appeal "present your bodies as a living sacrifice, holy and acceptable to God, which is your spiritual worship" (Rom 12:1); this new form of Christian worship is made possible by sharing in Jesus' love and being incorporated into his body

2. Saint Paul expresses the same idea when he speaks of "the priestly service of the gospel" and its aim to make an "offering" of the Gentiles (Rom 15:15–16)

   a. True worship is the living person shaped by God's transforming word, and true priesthood is a ministry of word and sacrament that transforms others into an offering

   b. The heart of apostolic ministry, then, is drawing people into union with the perfect sacrifice of the Cross

   c. A further dimension of Christian worship when he describes his anticipated martyrdom as a sacrificial event

      1) His life will be poured out as "a libation upon the sacrificial offering of your faith" (Phil 2:17)

      2) Martyrdom too draws one into the liturgy of the Cross

   d. This same understanding that suffering and love make us an offering to God is evident in the accounts of the martyrdom of Saints Ignatius of Antioch, Polycarp, and Lawrence

Questions for Understanding

1. The Synoptic Gospels (Matthew, Mark, and Luke) tell us that the veil of the Temple was torn in two as Jesus died on the Cross. What two important truths does this event signify according to Benedict (pp. 209–10)?

2. Psalm 22 is fundamental to the Passion story. What are some of the details of the psalm that anticipate the crucifixion scene? In what ways does the psalm point beyond the events of Good Friday into the age of the Church? Also, how does the Pope explain the significance of Jesus' cry of abandonment, which is a quotation from the first line of the psalm (pp. 213–16)?

3. Benedict refers to the episode in John 19:25–27, where Jesus entrusts his Mother to the care of the beloved disciple, as a kind of "adoption arrangement" (p. 220). What is the meaning of Jesus' gesture at the human level (pp. 220–21)? What is its deeper significance (pp. 221–22)? What in Jesus' words suggests this?

4. To ensure that Jesus died on the Cross, a soldier thrust a spear into his side "and at once there came out blood and water" (Jn 19:34). What two interpretations did the Church Fathers give to this event (p. 226)? What is the significance of Christ's being pierced rather than having his legs broken, as was customary (pp. 225–26)?

5. Some people object to the idea of atonement on the grounds that only a cruel God would demand such a thing. How does Benedict respond (p. 232)?

6. Pope Benedict explains the crucifixion in terms of Jesus' incarnate obedience. What did his fulfillment of the Father's will accomplish for us (pp. 233–35)? Why was Jesus' human obedience to God's word necessary?

Questions for Application

1. It is remarkable the number of Old Testament references that appear in the Gospel accounts of the Passion. How does recognizing some of these scriptural texts add depth to your understanding of the events? List two Old Testament passages identified by Pope Benedict that you never saw before. How have these opened your eyes to see new dimensions of meaning in the Gospels?

2. When Jesus begs forgiveness for those who crucified him, he says "they know not what they do" (Lk 23:34). According to Benedict, how can ignorance sometimes prepare us to receive the Lord's blessings? By the same token, how can expert knowledge sometimes be a barrier to seeing God at work in the world? Consider your answer in light of Saint Paul's autobiographical comments in 1 Timothy 1:13.

3. Contemplating the thief on the cross, Benedict states: "God's mercy can reach us even in our final moments" and "even after a misspent life" (p. 212). All of us can take comfort in these words as we anticipate the end of our lives. But perhaps you know someone who is refusing to reconcile with God. Does the Pope's statement encourage you to take steps to entrust that person to the Lord's mercy? What steps are you (or would you consider) taking?

4. While suffering on the Cross, Jesus gives his Mother into the care of the beloved disciple (Jn 19:25–27). Benedict draws from this the following application: "Again and again the [Christian] disciple is asked to take Mary as an individual and as the Church into his own home and, thus, to carry out Jesus' final instruction" (p. 222). Name some specific ways one can do this as a faithful follower of Christ.

5. Benedict speaks of the "existential dimension" of the Cross (p. 236) and finds a lucid expression of it in Romans 12:1–2. After consulting this passage, ask yourself: What is the practical meaning of Paul's injunction to offer your body as a living sacrifice? If Jesus already did this on our behalf, then why is sacrifice asked of his followers? How might this relate to Benedict's description of the Cross as the perfect act of worship?

Terms

Christ-event, 204
corporate personality, 215
Dies Irae, 213
Emmaus, 203

hilastērion, 231
ne plus ultra, 223
post factum, 211

Notes

CHAPTER NINE

Jesus' Resurrection from the Dead

Summary

The Resurrection of Jesus is the foundation of Christianity. The Church's faith "stands or falls" with the truth of the Apostles' testimony to this event. In fact, the figure of Jesus may be said to stand or fall on this basis as well. For if Jesus lies dead in a tomb, then he was a failed religious leader with no ultimate claim on our lives; but if he is truly risen, then God has revealed himself in the world and mankind's situation has been forever changed.

Scripture describes the Resurrection as something new and unprecedented. It was a real and tangible event of history, but it was no mere resuscitation of a corpse. The New Testament shows us that Jesus has risen to a new life that is beyond the reach of death, and in doing so he has opened the way to a new dimension of existence for all humanity. Benedict explains that the glory of Easter Sunday exceeded even Jewish hopes for a general resurrection at a future time when the world itself would be renewed. Christ has been raised in the midst of the old world that still experiences death and decay, yet with a body that is no longer limited by the laws of nature as we know them. Scholars sometimes claim that such an idea conflicts with modern science. But the world studied by science is not called into question by the Resurrection; instead, a new horizon of reality, not previously known, has been stretched out before us.

The New Testament contains two primary forms of testimony regarding the Resurrection of Jesus: (1) the "confessional tradition" and (2) the "narrative tradition".

(1) *The confessional tradition.* The confessional tradition is expressed in formulas that distill the essential facts of the Resurrection and constitute a summary of the Church's faith. These confessions are fixed in their wording and have been considered binding from the beginning. Such confessions are found in Luke 24:34, Romans 10:9, and, most importantly, in 1 Corinthians 15:3–5.

In 1 Corinthians 15:3–5 Paul takes great care to transmit both the content and form of the earliest apostolic tradition. The essential facts of this ancient confession are set forth as the death, burial, and Resurrection of Jesus in fulfillment of the

Scriptures, along with a list of witnesses to the Resurrection. Benedict suggests this confession originated in Jerusalem in the 30s of the first century, at the very dawn of Christian history.

Christ's death is presented in 1 Corinthians 15:3–5 as something that fits into God's purpose revealed in Scripture. The affirmation that "Christ died for our sins" shows also that God lowered himself into our world with the aim of drawing us back to himself. The statement that Christ was "buried" is brief but also important. Jesus' placement in a tomb confirms his death. The empty tomb does not prove the Resurrection of Jesus, but it was a "necessary condition for Resurrection faith", contrary to what some theologians today claim. The Resurrection requires that the Lord's tomb was empty; otherwise, someone producing his dead body would have rendered the Church's proclamation impossible.

References to Jesus rising "on the third day" and appearing to "Cephas" (Peter) and to "the Twelve" are also significant, for the third day quickly became the Lord's day, the day of Christian assembly and worship, and his appearances to the Apostles—and to Peter first of all—confirms their mission to establish the Church by their testimony to these events.

(2) *The narrative tradition.* The narrative tradition consists of the Resurrection stories that are found in the Gospels and the Acts of the Apostles. These accounts differ from confessional statements by detailing the discovery of the empty tomb, by reporting various encounters with the risen Lord and the words he spoke on those occasions, and by underscoring the role of women as the first witnesses to his rising rather than just men.

Benedict looks first at the narrative of Christ's appearance to Paul on the Damascus road (recounted in Acts 9:1–9; 22:6–11; 26:12–18). This was a unique encounter, quite unlike those mentioned in the Gospels. Most important is the heavenly light that shone around Paul (Acts 26:13) and the heavenly voice (Acts 26:14) that commissioned him to announce the Gospel of salvation to the Gentiles. The event obviously had a profound impact on Paul. He was not only blinded by the brightness of the glorified Jesus, but he received insight into the profound unity between Jesus and the members of his Church (Acts 9:4, "Saul, Saul, why do you persecute me?").

In the Gospel accounts Jesus presents himself as a living man who is visible and touchable, yet whose physical existence is no longer bound by the laws of space and time. Curiously, he is not recognizable at first sight; the disciples are unexpectedly slow to identify him as Jesus (Lk 24:15–16). Nevertheless, their interior sense perceives the Lord in their midst (Jn 21:12). There is an analogy here with Old Testament manifestations of God (called "theophanies") or his angels in human form. In several of these episodes, one finds a similar dynamic between God's closeness and his otherness such that his presence is perceived inwardly rather than outwardly. In any case, the physical realism of the Resurrection is confirmed by actions such as Jesus taking food and sharing meals with his disciples (see Lk 24:30, 41–43; Acts 1:4).

The Resurrection of Jesus was truly historical but not merely historical. It involved a real event and allowed for real encounters with the living Christ that cannot be explained simply as mystical experiences. At the same time, the physical body of Jesus has crossed over into the sphere of God and his eternity. It has been transformed into a new "place"—what Paul calls "the body of Christ"—where men and women can now enter into lasting communion with the Father. That the Lord should reveal himself to a few chosen disciples and not to the world at large is part of the mystery of God. The Lord never seeks to overwhelm us with his power; rather, he works in gentle ways to show us his love and to elicit our free response of love in return.

Outline

I. What is the Resurrection of Jesus?

A. The importance of the Resurrection of Jesus

    1. Christianity stands or falls with the Resurrection of Jesus

    2. Only if Jesus is risen can he be the criterion of truth and confirmation that God has revealed himself

    3. Our stance on the Resurrection determines our stance on the figure of Jesus as such—who he was or is

B. What actually happened to Jesus?

    1. The disciples were overwhelmed by a reality that went beyond their experience

    2. Clarifying what "rising from the dead" means

       a. Rudolf Bultmann's objection that if Jesus rose from the grave a miraculously resuscitated dead man would be irrelevant to us

       b. Reply

          1) If the Resurrection of Jesus were a miraculous resuscitation, then it would ultimately be irrelevant because it would not change the general human condition

          2) The Resurrection of Jesus was not a resuscitation, as was the raising of the widow's son (Lk 7:11–17), Jairus' daughter (Mk 5:22–24), and Lazarus (Jn 11:1–44)

          3) The Resurrection of Jesus was a "breaking out" into an entirely new form of life, one beyond death and "becoming"

          4) The Resurrection of Jesus is a universal event that affects everyone and opens up a new future for mankind (analogous to an "evolutionary leap")

C. Understanding the unique character of the New Testament testimony regarding Jesus' Resurrection

1. Jesus' entirely new kind of life affects how the witnesses describe their encounters

2. Resurrection before the end of time was unexpected and initially unintelligible for the disciples

    a. Jewish expectation of a general resurrection at the end of time

    b. An individual resurrection in the midst of the old world required rethinking/rereading of Scripture akin to the rethinking/rereading required by a crucified Messiah

3. The disciples' rereading Scripture in light of the Resurrection presupposes it was as real for them as the Cross; they could not ignore what they had seen and heard

4. The paradox of the Resurrection: something beyond the realm of normal human experience, yet undeniable as a real and tangible event

D. Certain kinds of modern thought reject the possibility of the Resurrection

1. Some thinkers such as Gerd Lüdemann claim the scientific world view excludes the Resurrection

2. But the Resurrection does not conflict with scientific data, but it goes beyond the present order of human existence

3. The Lord's appearances to a chosen few: a small beginning, easily overlooked, but something truly great that alone accounts for the fearless testimony of the disciples

II. Two types of Resurrection testimony

A. The confessional tradition

1. Condensed formulas fixed in their wording and expressing Christian identity and faith (Lk 24:34; Rom 10:9; 1 Cor 15:3–8)

2. 1 Corinthians 15:3–5 the most important Easter confession

    a. Background concerning the confession

        1) Paul faithfully transmits the Church's common tradition, preserving even its literal wording

        2) Paul extends the confession of faith by listing additional witnesses to the Resurrection, including James, over five hundred witnesses, "all" the Apostles, and Paul himself

    b. Key elements of the confession: Jesus' death, the empty tomb, the third day, the witnesses

1) Jesus' death

    a) Understanding Jesus' death through the lens of Scripture: the unfolding of the divine plan

    b) His death "for our sins", not as a consequence of man's original sin that brings death to all, but as an expression of God's humility that brings reconciliation

2) The question of the empty tomb

    a) The empty tomb is not enough to prove the Resurrection because there would be other explanations

    b) Some commentators jump to the conclusion that the empty tomb is irrelevant

    c) Benedict's conclusion: the empty tomb is an insufficient but necessary condition for Resurrection faith

    d) Paul's confessional statement presupposes the empty tomb

        (1) The statement "he was buried" certifies that Jesus really died and presupposes an empty tomb

        (2) In the earliest Christian preaching bodily corruption is incompatible with the notion of resurrection (e.g., Acts 2:26–29)

        (3) Modern speculations that Jesus' body may have decomposed contradicts the biblical vision of what "resurrection" means

3) The third day: the raising of Jesus took place "in accordance with the Scriptures", though no direct scriptural testimony specifies its occurrence on "the third day"

    a) The expression is not derived from Hosea 6:1–2

    b) It is the day of the first encounters with the risen Jesus

    c) It is the day when the early Christians assembled for worship (see Acts 20:7; 1 Cor 16:2; Rev 1:10)

    d) Because of the Resurrection, the first day of the week (Sunday) replaces the customary Sabbath observance (Saturday)

4) The witnesses

    a) Jesus appeared to "Cephas" (i.e., Peter) and to "the Twelve"; indicates that belief in the Resurrection is a basic tenet of apostolic tradition

    b) The initial appearance to Cephas renews his mission as the "rock" on which the Church is built; similar emphasis on Peter's role evidenced in John's Gospel (Jn 21:15–17)

B. The Narrative Tradition

    1. The narrative tradition involves various accounts of resurrection appearances linked with various bearers of tradition

        a. The different appearances can be divided between locations in Galilee and Jerusalem

        b. Notable differences of detail in reports regarding encounters among the four Gospels are summarized

        c. The abrupt ending of Mark's Gospel remains explained, though it too presupposes the empty tomb and Resurrection appearances

    2. General differences between the narrative tradition and the confession tradition

        a. Narratives relate encounters with the risen Jesus, the words he spoke, and the testimony of women, which is prominent: confessional formulas establish the key facts and follow juridical norms by naming only men as witnesses

        b. Narratives describe as well as report the risen Lord's appearances

            1) Jesus' appearances to Paul

                a) Three accounts of Paul's encounter with the risen Christ in the Acts of the Apostles; narratives focus on the "light" that shone around Paul and the "voice" that spoke to him (Acts 26:13–14)

                b) Jesus identifies himself with the persecuted Church (Acts 9:4) and entrusts Paul with a mission to enlighten Israel and the Gentiles (Acts 26:16–18)

            2) The appearances of Jesus in the Gospels different from Paul's encounter: Jesus appears as an embodied man, yet initially he is unrecognized in many accounts

                a) In the Emmaus story (Lk 24:13–35), in the appearance to Mary Magdalene (Jn 20:11–18), and at the Lake of Gennesaret (Jn 21:1–14)

                b) This reflects a dialectic of recognition and nonrecognition, of identity and otherness

                c) This pattern of nonrecognition and recognition supports the veracity of the Resurrection accounts

                d) Analogy of Old Testament theophanies, in which the Lord's presence is recognized from within (his appearances to Abraham) or at the moment of his disappearance (stories of Gideon and Samson); although Jesus presents himself as a true man, not simply under the appearance of a man

3. Complementary aspects of Jesus' resurrected existence

    a. Jesus lives anew in fellowship with God beyond death, yet the disciples have a real encounter with an embodied person, not a ghost

    b. Luke's presentation of Jesus' embodiment (Lk 24:36–43)

        1) Most exegetes who think Luke is exaggerating the physicality of Jesus and contradicting his own depiction of Jesus' Resurrection

        2) Benedict's reply considers three texts in which the risen Jesus participates in a meal: Luke 24:31; John 21:1–14; and Acts 1:3–4

        3) Jesus' "eating salt" with his disciples prior to his Ascension: drawing them into a new covenant-fellowship

        4) Link to the celebration of the Eucharist

III. Summary: The nature and historical significance of Jesus' Resurrection

A. Summary of Resurrection faith

    1. Jesus did not rise again to a normal biological life subject to death

    2. Jesus is not a ghost or spirit who belongs to the realm of the dead

    3. Jesus' appearances are not mystical experiences but real encounters with a living person

B. The true nature of Christ's Resurrection

    1. It is a historical event, yet a transcendent event that reveals a new dimension of human existence

    2. Matter itself is taken up into eternal communion with God

    3. The resurrected body of Christ is also the place where man enters into an indestructible union with God

    4. The Resurrection of Jesus is an eschatological event that "points beyond history but has left a footprint within history"

    5. Only a real encounter with the risen Christ can satisfactorily explain the passion and boldness of the Apostles' preaching

C. The Resurrection and the mystery of God

    1. The Lord's way is not to overwhelm us with his power, but to work gently and inconspicuously within history so as to elicit love

    2. The Apostles' preaching could not have succeeded unless the power of truth was in their message

Questions for Understanding

1. According to Pope Benedict, what difference does it make if Jesus did not actually rise from the dead (pp. 241–42)? How does the nature of Christ's Resurrection differ from the resuscitation of a corpse (pp. 243–45)?

2. Similar to the crucifixion of Jesus, which at first made no sense to the disciples, the Resurrection of Jesus was initially unintelligible. Why was this the case, given that a belief in bodily resurrection had already been a part of the Jewish faith (pp. 245–46)? What aspect of Christ's rising from the dead was unforeseen (pp. 245–46)?

3. Benedict refers to the Resurrection event as "the smallest mustard seed of history" (p. 247). What does he mean by this? In what sense can this mighty act of God on Easter morning be called "small"?

4. The confessional creed that Paul transmits in 1 Corinthians 15:3–5 states that Christ both died and rose again "in accordance with the scriptures". What passages from the Old Testament does Benedict provide as pointing to these two great events (pp. 252–53)? Can you think of any others that might be assumed in the statement?

5. Some modern theologians attempt to define the Resurrection of Jesus without reference to his body coming to life again. How does Saint Peter's Pentecost sermon in Acts 2:14–36 show that the early Christians thought otherwise about the nature of a resurrection (pp. 255–57)? Why, according to Benedict, was it so important for the early Church to stress that Christ's body did not undergo corruption (pp. 256–57)?

6. How does the early Christian observance of the first day of the week, Sunday, as the Lord's day indicate that an extraordinary event must have occurred on that day (p. 259)?

7. The disciples initially failed to recognize the resurrected Jesus. He was clearly the same man as before, and yet he was also a new man. How, in Benedict's estimation, does this fact add to the credibility of the Resurrection stories? How might these accounts have read differently if the Resurrection was simply invented (pp. 266–67)?

8. How is Jesus' Resurrection life different from that of a ghost or spirit (pp. 268–69)?

9. How is the Resurrection of Jesus unlike other historical events (p. 275)? How is it like other historical events (p. 275)?

Questions for Application

1. If you think about it, the entirety of Catholic life and liturgy depends upon the historical truth of the Resurrection. What particular forms of worship and spirituality are made possible by Jesus rising with an immortal body? How does this give you a new appreciation for the Church's grand celebration of Easter?

2. Imagine you were a Jewish Christian in the first century, and from childhood you have been taught to observe every Sabbath day as a holy day. Beyond that, it was the cultural tradition to maintain this observance for centuries on the belief that God commanded it through Moses. How would you explain the newly established Christian custom of observing the Lord's day? How certain would you have to have been of the Resurrection to justify such a momentous shift in religious tradition? Consider your answer in light of Benedict's comments on the Lord's day (pp. 258–59).

3. Have you ever seen in person or in photographs an Incorruptible, a deceased saint whose body remains intact? How might these instances help you to explain and defend the Church's belief in Christ's Resurrection?

4. Benedict refers to the post-Resurrection meals that Jesus shared with his disciples as "self-manifestations of the risen Lord" (p. 271). What form does this table fellowship take in the ongoing life of the Church? How might it broaden or enhance our appreciation for the Eucharist to think of Jesus, not only as the food that is placed before us, but as the host who invites us to the feast and who serves us at table?

Terms

Blank, Josef, 258
Conzelmann, Hans, 257
evolutionary leap, 244
Gese, Hartmut, 246
Lüdemann, Gerd, 246

Schwemer, Anna Maria, 257
Söding, Thomas, 254
Tertullian, 274
theophanies, 267

He Ascended into Heaven—

He Is Seated at the Right Hand of the Father, and He Will Come Again in Glory

Summary

The Lord appeared to his disciples for a limited time after the Resurrection. These final days were spent readying them for their mission to tell the world that "Jesus is alive". The Apostles' first task was to summon Israel to faith in Christ. Ultimately, however, they were sent forth as bearers of the good news for "all nations" (Mt 28:19).

Included in their preaching was the announcement that Jesus will come again to establish the kingdom of God fully and forever. Many modern theologians claim that the "imminent expectation" of the kingdom and Jesus' return was the main message of the early Christians. Benedict rejects this claim, asking how Christianity could have survived such an unfulfilled expectation. The thesis contradicts the textual evidence of early Christian belief and history. More than anything else, the earliest generations bore witness to the present reality that the resurrected Jesus lives, who now brings new life to the world.

But if Jesus is present now, in the new life he offers, what is the meaning of the promise of his return? How should we understand his present "absence"? The accounts of Jesus' Ascension provide the answer.

Luke's telling of the event is surprising: immediately after Jesus was "carried up into heaven" his disciples returned to Jerusalem "with great joy" (Lk 24:51–52). Why joy rather than sadness? The disciples did not feel abandoned: they were convinced of Jesus' new and permanent presence.

In the Acts of the Apostles Jesus is taken up in a "cloud" (Acts 1:9). This event signals Jesus' "entry into the mystery of God". Jesus' destination, described in the language of Psalm 110:1, is the right hand of God. This does not refer to a journey to some distant cosmic place. God is not limited to being present in one place; he is the transcendent Lord of all space. "Sitting at God's right hand" means sharing "in this divine dominion over space" (p. 283). The risen Jesus has ascended into communion with the life and power of the Father, who is present and accessible to all people of all times.

Benedict finds this truth beautifully illustrated in the Gospel story where Jesus leaves his disciples to pray on a mountain, only to come to them in their time of need on the sea (Mk 6:45–52). He regards this as an "image for the time of the Church" (p. 284).

Still more insight emerges from the first Resurrection appearance to Mary Magdalene (Jn 20:11–18). Initially, she does not recognize the risen Christ; but once he speaks her name, she wants to embrace him. However, Jesus responds, "Do not hold me, for I have not yet ascended to the Father" (Jn 20:17). This is surprising since one would expect that touching Jesus would be impossible once he withdrew from the world in his risen body. Benedict explains this to mean that the old manner of relating to Jesus no longer applies; for when Christ enters into communion with the Father, he becomes accessible to us in a new way. Through the new life of Baptism we are already with Christ in heaven (Col 3:1; see also Eph 2:6).

Belief in the second coming is also a part of the Christian confession of faith. It includes the hope that suffering will pass away, that every wrong will be righted in the end, and that the "triumph of love will be the last word of world history" (p. 287). In the meantime, Christians are called to a state of vigilance. Turning our focus beyond the present moment and its concerns, we must order our lives according to the truth and goodness of God. Furthermore, Benedict urges us to pray for the Lord's return, just as the earliest believers did (see 1 Cor 16:22 and Rev 22:20).

Still, anticipating the Lord's coming does not exclude celebrating his presence among us here and now. Indeed, Jesus promised to be with his disciples "always" (Mt 28:20), and he is especially close to us in the Eucharist. Theologians such as Saint Bernard of Clairvaux speak of a threefold coming of Christ. Between the Lord's first coming in the flesh and his final coming in glory, Saint Bernard identifies a "middle coming" in spirit and in power. Jesus comes to the faithful even now through his word, in the sacraments, and through various words or events in our lives. He also comes to us in times of great spiritual renewal in history: for example, in the work of Saints Francis and Dominic in the medieval period, and in the lives of Saints Teresa of Avila, John of the Cross, Ignatius Loyola, and Francis Xavier in the sixteenth century. Benedict bids us to pray for the coming of Jesus in all of its manifestations, that his presence will be effective in the Church and in history leading up to his final return.

Jesus ascends into heaven in an act of final blessing (see Lk 24:50–51). This gesture is a sign of Christ's continuing relationship with his followers and with the world. Ultimately, this explains how the disciples could rejoice at his departure, for Jesus stretches his hands out in blessing over us all.

Outline

I. Post-Resurrection appearances of the Lord and the mission of the Church

A. The Resurrection appearances of Jesus were for a limited time

B. Their purpose was to assemble a group of witnesses to proclaim Jesus' Resurrection and its meaning

   1. The mission of proclamation was initially directed to Israel

   2. The universal mission of proclamation to the world was later undertaken

C. A trend in recent theology sees the second coming as the main content of early Christian preaching

   1. If so, how did Christianity survive its unfulfilled expectation of an imminent return?

   2. Textual evidence of early preaching says otherwise

      a. Jesus' return was proclaimed but his Resurrection was the main message

      b. Jesus' living presence among Christians was emphasized

II. Ascension accounts help us understand Jesus' presence among his people

A. Luke 24:50–53 refers to the disciples' joy following Jesus' Ascension

   1. We would expect sadness at Jesus' departure

   2. The disciples' reaction of joy reveals their confidence in Jesus' abiding presence with them through his presence at God's right hand

   3. The Ascension is not the departure of Jesus to a distant place but a continuing presence that provides lasting joy

B. Acts 1:6–11 and the Ascension of Jesus

   1. The conversation between Jesus and his disciples before his Ascension

      a. The conversation about Jesus' restoring the Davidic kingdom

      b. Jesus rejects speculation over the future and promises power to carry out the disciples' mission of witness

   2. The meaning of Jesus' being taken up in a cloud

      a. The cloud represents the resurrected Jesus being taken up into the mystery of God and his dominion over space, not a journey through space

      b. Significant "cloud events"

         1) Transfiguration (Mt 17:5; Mk 9:7; Lk 9:34)

2) The "overshadowing" of Mary by the power of the Most High (Lk 1:35)

3) The presence of the Lord in the cloud in the tent (Ex 40:34)

4) The cloud that led the people of Israel in the wilderness (Ex 13:21–22)

3. Jesus' continued, intimate presence among his disciples

   a. Jesus has not departed altogether but is still present with us and for us

   b. John 14:28: Jesus speaks of leaving and returning to his disciples

   c. Jesus is no longer limited to being in a particular place but is now present and accessible to all, throughout time and space

   d. Mark 6:45–52 illustrates Jesus' being with the ever-present Father and therefore being with his disciples in their need

   e. The risen Jesus' encounter with Mary Magdalene (Jn 20:17): a change from a limited physical way of relating to Jesus to the unlimited communion with Jesus in his communion with the Father

   f. "Space travel" of the heart, from self-enclosed isolation to world-embracing divine love

III. The return of Jesus

A. The return of Jesus is the second pillar of the Christian confession; it anticipates God's being "all in all" through Christ and the end of all suffering

B. The call to vigilance in the "interim time" before the return of Christ

C. Our attitude toward the Lord's return

   1. Should we expect him or do we prefer not to?

   2. Early Christian witnesses of expectation

   3. The compatibility of the Christian's eager expectation of Jesus' return and the Christian's joyful thankfulness of the Lord's abiding presence

D. The "middle coming" (*adventus medius*)

   1. Tradition of the twofold coming of Christ (e.g., Cyril of Jerusalem)

      a. Jesus' coming in the Incarnation

      b. Jesus' coming in the final judgment

   2. The idea of the threefold coming completes the tradition of the twofold coming

      a. Saint Bernard of Clairvaux's teaching about the "middle coming"

      b. The middle coming (*adventus medius*) or third coming: Jesus' coming to be among his disciples now: through his word, in the sacraments, and in words and events of life

    c. His "middle coming" in world-changing ways in the present age: the examples of great saints by whose actions "Christ entered anew into history"

E. Praying for Jesus' coming: prayer for Jesus' coming in diverse ways

F. Jesus' continued presence is blessing us in our mission to "open up the world to God": the lasting motive of Christian joy

Questions for Understanding

1. Benedict addresses whether the earliest Christians had an "imminent expectation" that Jesus would return right away (p. 279). Does he agree or disagree with this common view among scholars? Explain how he justifies his interpretation (pp. 279–80).

2. Why are the disciples joyful after Jesus' Ascension rather than sorrowful at his departure (pp. 280–81)?

3. How does Benedict understand the cloud that took Jesus out of the disciples' sight at the Ascension (p. 282)?

4. Pope Benedict explains that Jesus did not ascend to a literal throne in the outer regions of the cosmos (pp. 282–83). Where, then, did he go (pp. 282–83)? What does the throne at God's right hand, mentioned in Psalm 110:1, actually signify (pp. 282–83)?

5. How does the story of Jesus praying to the Father on a mountain (Mk 6:45–52) anticipate the kind of closeness Jesus has with his disciples after the Ascension (pp. 284–85)?

6. When the risen Jesus first appears to Mary Magdalene, he says, "Do not hold me, for I have not yet ascended to the Father" (Jn 20:17). According to Benedict, what is so surprising about these words (p. 285)? How does he interpret them? Can you think of other ways, not mentioned by the Pope, in which we can "touch" the ascended Lord?

7. Explain what Saint Bernard of Clairvaux meant by the threefold coming of Christ (pp. 290–91). According to Benedict, how was the "middle coming" in Saint Bernard's scheme anticipated by Saint Augustine (p. 291)? What imagery did the latter use to expound this truth (p. 291)?

8. How are great saints such as Francis, Dominic, Teresa of Avila, John of the Cross, Ignatius of Loyola, and Francis Xavier examples of Jesus' "middle coming"?

Questions for Application

1. Benedict says that speculating about history and looking ahead into the unknown future are "not fitting attitudes for a disciple" (p. 282). That being so, how should we respond to persons or groups who claim to predict when the world will end? Do you think Jesus' words in Acts 1:7 have a bearing on predictions of divine intervention that come from alleged apparitions or locutions?

2. According to the Pope, vigilance is the responsibility laid upon Christians in the intervening time between the first and second comings of Christ. What exactly does vigilance mean? What are some ways we can break free from the pressing concerns of this world in order to maintain focus on the Lord?

3. The earliest Christians were fervent in praying, "Come, Lord Jesus!" (Rev 22:20). Is this practice a regular part of your own prayer life? If not, why not? In what situations are you most likely to yearn for Christ's return?

4. Saint Bernard of Clairvaux draws attention to the fact the Jesus comes to us even now. Have you ever thought about the proclamation of Scripture or the Lord's presence in the Eucharist as various "comings" of Jesus to his Church? How are these events similar and yet dissimilar to the awaited second coming?

Terms

Notes

Glossary

Abba. Aramaic word for "father" used by Jesus to address God (Mk 14:36). It reflects God's unique relationship to Jesus. Paul also uses it as a way Christians address God in prayer (Rom 8:15; Gal 4:6). Some scholars hold that the word reflects an intimate form of address a small child would use for his father.

Abomination that makes desolate. An act of sacrilege that profaned the Jerusalem Temple (see Dan 9:27; 11:31; 12:11). In the Book of Daniel, it refers to the seizure and profanation of the sanctuary by Antiochus Epiphanes in 167 B.C. Jesus used the expression in his eschatological discourse (Mt 24:15; Mk 13:14; translated "desolating sacrilege" in the RSV) to refer to a future sign for people to flee Jerusalem. Many commentators understand the sign to have been the Roman desecration of the Temple in A.D. 70. Pope Benedict does not reject this view, but he mentions another theory—that the "abomination that makes desolate" was taken to be the appointment of the former high priest Annas II, in A.D. 66, as a Jewish military leader against the Romans. In A.D. 62, Annas decreed the death of James, "the brother of the Lord" and leader of Jewish Christians. According to Benedict, Christians may have seen Annas' military appointment as the sign to flee Jerusalem.

Adventus medius. Latin expression meaning "the middle coming". It is used by Saint Bernard of Clairvaux in reference to the various ways, spiritual and sacramental, that Christ comes to the Church in the time between his first coming in the flesh and his final coming in glory.

Agápē. One of several Greek terms meaning "love". Christians have taken up the word to use for the kind of others-regarding, self-donating love that Jesus expressed in going to the Cross. In theology it is often translated "charity".

Antiochus IV. Ruler of the Seleucid Empire (Syria) from 175 B.C. until his death in 163 B.C. Also known as Antiochus Epiphanes (Greek, "manifest divine one"). He invaded Jerusalem in 167 B.C., set up an altar to Zeus Olympios in the Temple (2 Mac 6:2), and there sacrificed swine. The Book of Daniel (9:27; 11:31; 12:11) and 1 Maccabees 1:54 refer to this incident.

Apostolic succession. Theological term that refers to the continuation of those aspects of the Apostles' ministry capable of being passed on to successive generations of Christians. The expression is used by Benedict to refer to the "sacramental" continuation in the mission that originates with Jesus and continues in the specially designated witnesses. More specifically, it refers to the handing on of the authority to teach, sanctify, and govern to bishops (*Catechism of the Catholic Church*, nos. 77 and 861).

Augustine, Saint. Bishop, theologian, and Doctor of the Church (A.D. 354–430), sometimes called the "Second Founder of the Faith" because of his vast theological, pastoral, and literary contribution to Christianity.

Bar Kochba. Simon Bar Kochba (meaning "son of the star" in Aramaic); led a revolt against Roman occupation of Judea in A.D. 132. He succeeded in his initial attempt and for three years ruled Judea as an independent country, after which time the Romans took back Judea and Bar Kochba was defeated. He consciously presented himself as a Messianic figure.

Barabbas. Political revolutionary whose agitations the Romans put down. The crowds intimidated Pontius Pilate into releasing Barabbas, a political Messianic figure, instead of Jesus (Mt 27:15–21; Mk 15:6–11; Lk 23:13–18; Jn 18:39–40). "Barabbas" is Aramaic for "son of the father".

Barrett, Charles K. New Testament scholar (b. 1917); emeritus professor of divinity at the University of Durham.

Baumert, Norbert. Jesuit and professor emeritus of New Testament theology at the Sankt Georgen Graduate School of Philosophy and Theology in Germany. He is coauthor, with Maria-Irma Seewann, of an important article on the meaning of Jesus' words "for many" used at the Last Supper.

Benedictus. Latin term meaning "blessed" and used to identify part of the Latin liturgy of the Mass that draws on the phrase shouted by the crowd as Jesus entered Jerusalem: "Blessed is who comes in the name of the Lord" (Mt 21:9).

Berakah. The Hebrew term for "blessing". It often refers to a Jewish prayer formula used for praise and thanksgiving. Examples can be found in the Old Testament (1 Chron 29:10–13; Ps 135:21; Dan 3:3–68) as well as the New Testament (Lk 1:68–79; Eph 1:3–10).

Bernard of Clairvaux, Saint. Cistercian abbot, theologian, and Doctor of the Church (1090–1153). Benedict draws attention to Bernard's concept of "the middle coming" of Jesus in the age of the Church.

Blank, Josef. German Catholic biblical scholar (1926–1989) and the author of a book on Paul and Jesus (1968) in which the meaning of the confessional formula in 1 Corinthians 15:3–5 is discussed.

Bonhoeffer, Dietrich. German Lutheran theologian and pastor (1906–1945) executed for his anti-Nazi activities. He was critical of the idea of "cheap grace", too-easy forgiveness. His book *The Cost of Discipleship* stresses the demands of being a follower of Christ in the difficulties of "real life".

Book of Jubilees. A Jewish religious text from the second century B.C. It retells the biblical story from Creation to the Exodus, embellishing it with traditional elements said to have been revealed to Moses. Distinctive of the book is its conception of time: it divides history into 49-year Jubilee cycles and follows a 364-day solar calendar (instead of the 354-day liturgical calendar used in the Temple of Jerusalem).

Bouyer, Louis. Prolific French theologian and former Lutheran minister (1913–2004) who entered the Catholic Church in 1939. He was a leading twentieth-century figure in the Catholic biblical and liturgical movements, and he influenced the Second Vatican Council. Pope Benedict refers to Father Bouyer's efforts to trace the development of the Christian eucharistic liturgy from the Jewish *berakah*.

Brandon, Samuel George Frederick. British Anglican religious scholar and minister (1907–1971) best known for his work on comparative religion and for his thesis that Jesus was a political revolutionary shaped by the Zealots.

Brem, Hildegard. Cistercian and abbess of the Abbey of Maria-Stern Gwiggen (1951–present).

Brown, Raymond E. Sulpician priest and American biblical scholar (1928–1998). Benedict refers to his magisterial *Anchor Bible* commentary on the Gospel of John, in which Brown supports the historicity of Jesus' dialogue with Pontius Pilate on the true nature of his kingship (Jn 18:33–38).

Bultmann, Rudolf. German Protestant biblical scholar and theologian (1884–1976) who attempted to "de-mythologize" Christianity—to separate what he considered the essence of Christianity from the world view of the scriptural authors, which he regarded as mythological. Bultmann was also among the leading proponents of "form criticism". He also maintained that the Gospels were not historical narratives but theology reshaped into the form of a story. He believed that Christianity needed to be understood in terms of the early philosophy of Martin Heidegger rather than what he regarded as the mythical world view of the biblical writers.

Caiaphas. The Jewish high priest from A.D. 18 to 36. During this time he also presided over the Jewish high court, the Sanhedrin. The Gospels remember Caiaphas as the one who counseled the Jerusalem leadership that Jesus should die instead of the people (Jn 11:49–52) and who eventually declared him guilty of blasphemy (Mt 27:62; Mk 14:61). He was the son-in-law of the former high priest Annas, who also examined Jesus on the night of his arrest (Jn 18:13, 19–24).

Canon of Scripture. The collection of sacred writings regarded as divinely inspired and therefore authoritative expressions of Christian faith. It consists of the books of the Old Testament and the books of the New Testament.

Caritas. Latin word meaning "sacrificial love or charity".

Christ-event. A shorthand expression for the redemptive actions of Jesus in history. As used by scholars, it typically includes the full sweep of his Incarnation and public ministry as well as his death, Resurrection, and Ascension.

Christology. The branch of theology concerned with the person, nature, and activity of Christ.

Christology from above. An approach to the study of Christ that begins with the facts of his divinity and preexistence and that draws conclusions about how these realities affected his historical experience as a man—as one person having a human as well as a divine nature.

Christology from below. An approach to the study of Christ that begins with a historical investigation of what can be known about the words and deeds of Jesus and the early Church's understanding of them.

Church Fathers. Saintly Christian writers who lived in the early centuries of the Church and whose writings have a special place in the understanding of normative Christian beliefs and practices; also known as "the Fathers of the Church".

Chytraeus, David. Moderate German Lutheran theologian (1531–1600). He taught at the University of Rostock, was a pupil of Philip Melanchthon, and was one of the coauthors of the Lutheran statement of faith, the Formula of Concord (1577). He coined the expression "high-priestly prayer" for Jesus' prayer to the Father in John 17.

Collins, Francis S. Contemporary American geneticist (b. 1950) and current director of the National Institutes of Health. In 2009 Pope Benedict XVI appointed him to the Pontifical Academy of Sciences. He is author of *The Language of God*, in which he argues for a compatibility of science and religion.

Conzelmann, Hans. German New Testament scholar and redaction critic (1915–1989). Benedict agrees with Conzelmann's assessment that Hosea 6:1–2 is not, in the first instance, a text about the Resurrection of Jesus "on the third day" (1 Cor 15:4).

Corporate personality. The theological idea, based on Old Testament notions, that a group is represented by an individual who "personifies" some aspect of the group's nature or by whom the group as a whole acts.

Council of Chalcedon. The Fourth Ecumenical Council of the Church (A.D. 451). It is famous for its Christological definition that Jesus Christ is one person in two natures, one human and one divine, without the two natures being confused or separated.

Council of Nicea. An assembly of Catholic bishops that met in A.D. 325. It rejected Arianism, which claimed that Jesus was not fully divine. Instead, it taught that Jesus was "begotten", not created. The Council of Nicea is the First Ecumenical Council of the Church.

Cyril of Jerusalem, Saint. Bishop and theologian as well as Father and Doctor of the Church (d. 387). Around A.D. 350 Cyril delivered a series of *Catechetical Lectures* that are famous for summarizing the fundamentals of Christian doctrine for catechumens.

David. Celebrated psalmist, successor to King Saul, and the first to reign as king over all the tribes of Israel (ca. 1010 to 970 B.C.). The heart of Jewish Messianism was the belief that God's anointed deliverer would be a royal descendant of David (cf. Is 9:6–7; Jer 23:5–6; Ezek 34:23–24).

Day of Atonement/Feast of Atonement. One of the principal liturgical feasts of Israel held annually on the tenth day of the seventh month (Lev 16:1–34). It is known today in Hebrew as *Yom Kippur*. In ancient Israel, its purpose was twofold: to cleanse the sanctuary from ritual impurity and to atone for the sins of the priests and people accumulated throughout the preceding year. The latter is linked with the rite of the scapegoat, by which the sins of Israel were "offloaded" onto a goat that symbolically bore them away into the wilderness (Lev 16:20–22). Christians see in Jesus' death the accomplishment for mankind of what the Day of Atonement represents.

Day of Preparation. The day before the Jewish Passover (Jn 19:14). The Passover lambs were slaughtered on this day so they could be consumed in the evening Passover meal. Pope Benedict follows most scholars in identifying the afternoon of Good Friday as the vigil of the Passover. Thus, Jesus was crucified as "the Lamb of God" on the afternoon when Passover lambs were being slaughtered in the Temple.

Didachē. Early Christian writing, also known as the *Teaching of the Twelve Apostles*, thought to have been written ca. A.D. 70–120. The name of the book comes from the Greek word meaning "teaching".

Didascalia Apostolorum. A Christian treatise, the title of which means the "teaching of the apostles", dating from the third century and preserved mainly in Syriac. The document places the Last Supper and arrest of Jesus on Tuesday evening of Holy Week rather than on the traditional Thursday evening.

Dies Irae. A medieval Latin hymn entitled "the Day of Wrath". Its poetic lines are based in part on the words of Zephaniah 1:15–16, and its subject is the fearful prospect of standing before Christ at the Last Judgment.

Dodd, Charles H. British Protestant New Testament scholar (1884–1973) who espoused a "realized eschatology", the idea that the kingdom of God is a present reality. Dodd's best-known work is *The Interpretation of the Fourth Gospel* (1953). Pope Benedict agrees with Dodd's support for the historic authenticity of Jesus' exchange with Pilate regarding Jesus' kingly identity.

Dominic, Saint. Spanish founder of the Order of Preachers, popularly known as the Dominicans (1170–1221). Dominic is also remembered for his efforts as a zealous evangelist and defender of Catholic orthodoxy against the heresy of Albigensianism.

Ecce homo. Latin form of the words meaning "Behold the Man!" spoken by Pontius Pilate (Jn 19:5). Pilate's declaration came as he displayed the scourged Christ before the hostile mob.

Ecclesiology. The branch of theology concerned with the nature of the Church.

Ecumenical. A term referring to the promotion of Christian unity.

Ecumenical Council. A special assembly of the bishops of the universal Church, together with the bishop of Rome (the Pope), to address doctrinal and pastoral matters. There have been twenty-one Ecumenical Councils, according to the reckoning generally accepted in the Catholic Church.

Emmaus. A village seven miles west of Jerusalem. According to Luke 24:13–35, two disciples were traveling on foot to Emmaus on Easter Sunday when they were joined on the way by the risen Jesus. More than once Benedict draws lessons from this important episode.

Epiphanius of Salamis. Fourth-century Church Father and bishop known for his staunch defense of orthodox Christian belief against various heresies. Pope Benedict quotes Epiphanius' explanation for the Christians' flight to Pella beyond the Jordan before the siege of Jerusalem in A.D. 70. According to Epiphanius, Christians fled because they recalled Jesus' warning to abandon the city before its destruction.

Eschatology. The branch of theology concerned with the "last things" (Greek, *eschatos*, "last [things]") or the final destiny of man and the world.

Eschatological discourse. Name given to Jesus' discourse recorded in Matthew 24:3–24, Mark 13:3–37, and Luke 21:5–36. It is called "eschatological" because it refers to the divine judgment to come upon a disobedient Jerusalem (which came with the destruction of the Temple in A.D. 70) and because it anticipates the final judgment at the end of the world. Pope Benedict stresses three key elements of Jesus' discourse: the destruction of the Temple, the times of the Gentiles, and prophecy and apocalyptic teaching.

Essenes. A Jewish ascetical sect that existed in Palestine from the second century B.C. to the first Jewish revolt and fall of Jerusalem, ca. A.D. 66–70. Essenes probably made up the community at Qumran, with which the Dead Sea Scrolls are associated, although the sect also had members who lived elsewhere. The Essenes were critical of the religious establishment in Jerusalem, and they regarded the worship at the Temple as corrupt. They also anticipated an eschatological "showdown" between "the sons of light" (themselves) and "the sons of darkness", the enemies of God's righteous people.

Eternal life. Term used by Jesus to refer to the kind of life man may graciously come to possess in relationship with God, who is life. Eternal life (Greek, *zōē*) begins in this life through a person's knowing God and entering into communion with him through Jesus Christ.

Etiology of worship. A traditional story that explains the origin and founding of a particular form of worship and serves to legitimize it.

Evangelist. An author of one of the four Gospels of Matthew, Mark, Luke, and John.

Evolutionary leap. A term from biology used to describe the relatively rapid transition of an organism to a more highly evolved state. Benedict applies this concept analogously to the sudden perfection of human nature witnessed in the resurrected Jesus.

Exegesis. The process of interpreting what a text means.

Exegete. An expert who interprets the meaning of a text.

Exemplum. Latin term meaning "example". It appears in the Vulgate translation of John 13:15, where Jesus, having washed the feet of his disciples, urges them to follow his example of humble service to others. Benedict relates the example (*exemplum*) of Jesus to his gift of himself on the Cross, symbolically (*sacramentum*) anticipated in his washing of the disciples' feet. In this act, he not only gives the disciples an example to follow, but he empowers them to act and acts through them.

Exitus–reditus. Latin terms meaning "departure" and "return". Originally *exitus-reditus* referred to a construct of the Neoplatonist philosopher Plotinus (ca. A.D. 205–270), who envisioned man's emanation (or creation) from the divine as a fall into the bondage of the material order and his return as a struggle to free himself from matter. Pope Benedict contrasts this scheme with the evangelist's remark that Jesus "had come from God and was going to God" (Jn 13:3). Christ's descent in the Incarnation affirms the goodness of material creation, just as his bodily Ascension indicates that matter is destined for the presence of God.

Expiation. Theological term for the divine action of "taking away sins". Variously symbolized in the liturgical rites of the Old Testament, expiation occurs in a definitive way through the sacrifice of Jesus Christ (see Jn 1:29; Rom 3:24–25; Heb 2:17).

Factum est. Part of a phrase used in the Latin translation of John 1:14. The whole passage reads: "Verbum caro factum est et habitavit in nobis", meaning: "The Word was made flesh and dwelt among us." The term can be used more generally to refer to the historical reality of Jesus' life, death, and Resurrection.

Faith-hermeneutic. A term used by Pope Benedict to describe principles of interpreting the biblical texts from the perspective of faith.

Feast of Tabernacles. Also called the Feast of Booths, a biblical pilgrimage feast lasting seven days. Participants built temporary dwellings to recall the temporary dwellings the Israelites used in their forty-year sojourn in the desert after the Exodus (see Lev 23:33–36; Deut 16:13–15). Jesus gave his "rivers of living water" discourse (Jn 7:38) in the context of this feast (Jn 7:2, 37). Pope Benedict also connects the shout of "Hosanna", used by the priests at the feast, with the exclamation of the pilgrims accompanying Jesus into Jerusalem (Mt 21:9; Mk 11:9–10; Jn 12:13).

Feast of Unleavened Bread. A week-long Jewish festival celebrated in conjunction with the springtime Passover (Lev 23:4–8; Ezek 45:21). It commemorates the haste with which Israel escaped from Egypt, and no leavened bread was to be eaten throughout the seven days of the feast (Ex 12:14–20). Preparation was made on the eve of Passover by a ritual removal of leaven from every Israelite home (cf. 1 Cor 5:7). The Feast of Unleavened Bread forms part of the historical backdrop for the Last Supper (Mt 26:17; Mk 14:12; Lk 22:7–8).

Feuillet, André. Prominent French biblical scholar (1909–1998) whose work *The Priesthood of Christ and His Ministers* deeply informs Pope Benedict's interpretation of John 17:1–26. In particular, Feuillet's thesis that the high-priestly prayer of Jesus is modeled on the Day of Atonement liturgy generates rich theological reflections for the Pope that underscore the sacrificial dimensions of the Lord's Passion.

Fourth Gospel. The Gospel of John.

Francis, Saint. Italian founder of the Order of Friars Minor, popularly known as the Franciscans (1181–1226). Francis of Assisi is revered for his heroic embrace of poverty in imitation of Christ.

Francis Xavier, Saint. Spaniard and one of the founding members of the Society of Jesus (1506–1552). Beyond this, his principal accomplishments were as a missionary to India and Asia.

Gese, Hartmut. German Protestant Old Testament scholar (b. 1929). Benedict draws insights from an essay in Gese's book *Essays on Biblical Theology* (English translation, 1981).

Gnilka, Joachim. Contemporary Scripture scholar writing in German (b. 1928).

Guardini, Romano. Influential Italian-German theologian (1885–1968). He wrote on a wide variety of topics, including the liturgy and the historical character of Christian revelation. His book *The Lord* is a life of Jesus that inspired Benedict's *Jesus of Nazareth*.

Hallel Psalms. Psalms 113–18 and 136, which Jewish tradition prescribed for recitation at the yearly Passover. Pope Benedict suggests these may be the hymns sung by Jesus and the Apostles at the conclusion of the Last Supper (Mk 14:26). Insofar as these are psalms of thanksgiving for Israel's deliverance from Egypt, they also anticipate the new Passover deliverance that Jesus accomplishes through his death and Resurrection.

Harnack, Adolf von. German Protestant theologian and Scripture scholar (1851–1930) who helped establish the historical-critical method. He sought to "de-hellenize" Christianity by removing the influences of Greek thought and culture in order to "return" to what he regarded as a purer form of Christianity. He argued that Jesus' message focused on the Father and did not refer to himself. He also held that Hebrews 5:7 originally indicated that Jesus' prayer for deliverance from death was *not* heard by God.

Heidegger, Martin. German philosopher (1889–1976) who focused on the meaning of being. Heidegger greatly influenced major thinkers such as Jacques Derrida, Hans-Georg Gadamer, Leo Strauss, Jean-Paul Sartre, Hannah Arendt, and Karl Rahner, among many others. Bultmann assimilated Heidegger's philosophy in his eschatology, which allowed Bultmann to try to explain Christian faith in an eschatological context of standing ready for the challenge of the Gospel.

Hellenists. Mentioned in Acts 6:1 as a community of Jewish believers from the Diaspora who had resettled in Jerusalem. Their name is an indication that Greek was their first language rather than Hebrew or Aramaic. The first Christian martyr, Saint Stephen, is the best known of the Hellenists (Acts 6:5; 7:54–60).

Hengel, Martin. German scholar of religion (1926–2009) who focused on Christian and Jewish religions from 200 B.C. to A.D. 200. His scholarship undermines the influential position of Rudolf Bultmann that the sources of the Gospel of John are Gnostic rather than Jewish.

Hermeneutics. The branch of study concerned with principles of interpretation. Originally, the term was applied only to interpreting the Bible. Later it came to apply in general to methods of interpretation.

High priest. The chief religious representative of biblical Israel. He served as the primary mediator between God, to whom he interceded for the people with prayers and sacrifices, and the Israelite community, for whom he acquired blessings. In the New

Testament period, the high priest was also the acting head of the Jewish Sanhedrin. The Gospels refer by name to two high priests: Caiaphas, who occupied the office from A.D. 18 to 36 (Mt 26:57; Jn 11:49), and Annas, who had formerly held the position but was deposed by the Romans in A.D. 15 (Jn 18:13, 24).

High-priestly prayer. Traditional designation for Jesus' impassioned prayer to the Father in John 17:1–26. Benedict draws attention to four of its themes: the nature of eternal life, the sanctification of disciples in truth, the revelation of the Father's name, and the unity of believers.

Hilastērion. Greek term used in the Septuagint (LXX) Old Testament for the "mercy seat" or golden lid of the Ark of the Covenant (see Ex 25:17–22; Lev 16:2; Num 7:89). Benedict notes how Paul uses this term in Romans 3:25 (rendered "an expiation" in the RSVCE 2) to indicate that Christ crucified is the place of sacred contact between God and man that powerfully effects the remission of our sins. Paul is alluding to the Day of Atonement liturgy in which Israel's high priest sprinkled sacrificial blood on the mercy seat to secure forgiveness for the covenant people (Lev 16:14).

Historical-critical method. Broad term for a modern method of understanding biblical texts by drawing exclusively on the findings of the human sciences, including history, linguistics, philology, comparative literature, textual criticism, and archaeology. The method seeks primarily to know the meaning of a text as originally written and received. It does not presuppose the divine inspiration of the Bible or the truth of theology. Pope Benedict affirms the value of this method but cautions against its exclusive use or the unqualified acceptance of certain presuppositions of some of its users.

Historical hermeneutic. A principle of biblical interpretation that relies on historical criticism. Benedict maintains that when separated from certain ideas opposed to the faith, a historical hermeneutic can teach us about Jesus.

Historical Jesus. Either Jesus insofar as historians have been able to reconstruct him or Jesus as he really was in history. The distinction between the two senses of the term is based on the idea that historical scholarship cannot discover everything about a person. Often the term "Jesus of history" is used to refer to "Jesus as he really was in history". In this case, there would be a difference between the historical Jesus and the Jesus of history. Some scholars posit an opposition between "the historical Jesus", understood as "Jesus as he really existed", and the Christ of faith—Jesus as proclaimed by the Bible and the Church. Pope Benedict rejects the idea that "Jesus as he really was" is different from the Christ of faith. At the same time, Benedict acknowledges the limits of what historical methods alone can tell us about Jesus.

Historicity. Historical reality; that is, the degree to which something really happened as reported. Benedict insists on the historicity of the key Gospel events.

Hosanna. Hebrew term meaning "Save, we ask". Originally, it invoked the God of Israel's aid (Ps 118:25), and the Jewish liturgy of the Feast of Tabernacles used the term. "Hosanna" came to be used as an acclamation of praise as well as a supplication for God's saving help through the Messiah. The crowd used it to greet Jesus as he solemnly entered Jerusalem during the final week of his earthly life (Mt 21:9; Mk 11:9–10; Jn 12:13). The expression revealed the crowd's hope in Jesus as the Messiah. After Jesus' cleansing of the Temple, children in the Temple used the word to express their homage of Jesus as the Messiah (Mt 21:15).

Hour of Jesus. Term used in the Gospels, especially in John's Gospel, to refer to the time identified with Jesus' suffering, death, and Resurrection. Jesus refers to his "hour" as the time in which he, the Son of Man, is exalted and glorified (Jn 12:23; 17:1). He associates it with his departure from earthly existence to be with the Father (Jn 13:1), which entails Jesus' gift of himself out of love. Since Jesus' suffering and death are brought about by the forces of evil, Jesus' "hour" is also the time or "hour" of his enemies (Mt 26:45; Mk 14:41; Lk 22:53), who unwittingly contribute to Jesus' triumph.

Ignatius Loyola, Saint. Spanish founder of the Society of Jesus (1491–1556) and its first superior general (elected 1541). Ignatius is one of the Church's most celebrated converts from sinful to saintly living and is the author of a four-week course of meditations called *The Spiritual Exercises.*

Immanence. God's presence in creation, including his presence among his people. The fullness of God's immanence is found in Jesus Christ, who is "God-with-us". By the Incarnation, death, and Resurrection of the God-man, Jesus Christ, believers are united with God in the Holy Spirit to form the Church. The mission of the Church involves the transformation of the whole of creation through Jesus Christ. In this way, divine immanence is complemented by divine transcendence, which means that God transcends or exists outside of or beyond his creation.

Imminent expectation. A belief that the earliest Christian believers expected the return of Christ in glory to occur within their lifetime or shortly thereafter. Some New Testament scholars claim this expectation was the primary message of the early Church. Benedict acknowledges that the early Christians proclaimed the return of Christ as part of their message and that they often assumed the time until it occurred would be short. But he insists that the imminent coming of Jesus was not the primary Christian message. While believers looked forward to Jesus' return in glory, they affirmed his presence among them in the meantime. The main Christian message was that Jesus was alive through the Resurrection and makes new life available in the present.

Institution narratives. The accounts in the Synoptic Gospels (Mt 26:26–29; Mk 14:22–25; Lk 22:19–20) and 1 Corinthians (11:23–25) of Jesus' institution of the Eucharist at the Last Supper.

Ipsissima verba Iesu. Latin phrase meaning "the very words of Jesus". It refers to words Jesus himself spoke. The complementary expression is *ipsissima vox* of Jesus, which means "the very voice" of Jesus. The latter refers to words that express Jesus' ideas or meaning, rather than his exact words.

Jaubert, Annie. French scholar (1912–1980) best known for a theory accounting for the apparent discrepancies between the Synoptic Gospels (Matthew, Mark, and Luke) and the Gospel of John regarding whether the Last Supper took place on the evening of the Passover sacrifices or before it. According to Jaubert's theory, two different liturgical calendars were followed, one associated with the Essenes and the Qumran community, which placed the first day of Passover on Wednesday, and one recognized by the Jewish authorities, which placed the first day of Passover on Friday. Jesus and his disciples, on this view, participated in the Passover meal at the Last Supper according to the first calendar, on Tuesday night, while the Jewish authorities observed the Passover according to the second calendar, on Friday. Pope Benedict sympathetically summarizes Jaubert's theory without embracing it.

Jeremias, Joachim. German Lutheran Scripture scholar (1900–1979). He took a positive view of scholarship's ability to know the historical truth about Jesus. Jeremias taught the significance of Jesus' understanding of God as his Father, expressed by Jesus' use of the term "Abba". Jeremias also authored an important study of the eucharistic words of Jesus spoken during the Last Supper.

Jewish War, the. Sometimes also called the Jewish-Roman War or the First Jewish-Roman War, the term refers to the conflict between Jewish nationalists and the Roman authority in Palestine (ca. A.D. 66–70). The Roman legions under the general Titus crushed the rebellion and destroyed Jerusalem, its Temple, and the remaining rebel strongholds. The Jewish historian Flavius Josephus recounted the story of the conflict in *The Jewish War*. Jesus prophesied the Temple's destruction (Lk 20:5–6) and Jerusalem's conquest (Lk 20:21).

Johannine. Having to do with the Gospel of John or its author.

John of the Cross, Saint. Spanish mystic, Carmelite priest, and Doctor of the Church (1542–1591). Allied with Saint Teresa of Avila, he worked to reform the Carmelite Order and wrote several classic works of spiritual theology including *Dark Night of the Soul*.

Josephus, Flavius. Jewish historian (A.D. 37–ca. A.D. 100) who recorded the events of the Jewish War and the destruction of Jerusalem by the Roman armies.

Jungmann, J. A. Austrian theologian (1889–1975) best known for his work in liturgy and catechetics. He was a theological expert at the Second Vatican Council (1962–1965) and one of the architects of its Constitution on the Sacred Liturgy.

Pope Benedict refers to Jungmann's view that the Mass is the sacramental memorial of Jesus' sacrificial death, not a celebration of the Last Supper as such.

Kasper, Walter. German cardinal, Catholic theologian, and member of the Catholic Church's International Theological Commission (b. 1933). Among many church posts, he served as president of the Pontifical Council for Promoting Christian Unity. He is the author of a major book on Christology: *Jesus the Christ.*

Kattenbusch, Ferdinand. German Protestant theologian (1851–1935) perhaps best known for his book on the Apostles' Creed. Pope Benedict refers sympathetically to Kattenbusch's thesis that Jesus' words of institution at the Last Supper constitute the act of founding the Church.

Kingdom of God. God's reign. The kingdom of God is a major theme of Jesus' preaching (Mt 6:33; Mk 1:15; Lk 6:20) and includes the idea of the kingdom's presence in the person and ministry of Jesus (Lk 10:9; 17:21). The kingdom of God is present, but it awaits a fuller manifestation (Lk 13:29; 22:18) when Jesus shall reign as king (Mt 25:31, 34, 40; Lk 23:42). The kingdom of God is generally referred to as the kingdom of heaven in Matthew's Gospel (Mt 4:17). Some scholars contrast the message of the kingdom with the idea of Jesus' vicarious expiation of sin. They insist that the message of the kingdom is one of God's unconditional forgiveness and love, which they regard as at odds with the idea of an atoning sacrifice. Benedict insists that Jesus' love expressed by the offering of his cruel death for sin expresses God's unconditional forgiveness and love. God in Christ offers himself out of love despite all of man's rejection of him.

Knopf, Rudolf. German Christian scholar (1874–1920) and professor at the university of Bonn.

Kroll, Gerhard. German Jesuit priest and biblical scholar. Benedict relies on his work *Auf den Spuren Jesu* (*The Footsteps of Jesus* [5th edition, 1975]) for an accurate topographical description of Gethsemane.

Leo the Great, Saint. Fifth-century Pope and Doctor of the Church (d. A.D. 461). Benedict makes reference to Leo's *Tome*, a famous letter written to the bishop of Constantinople in 449 and read aloud at the Council of Chalcedon in 451. It distills with precision the Church's traditional doctrine on the one person and two natures of Christ.

Logikē latreía. Greek expression used by Saint Paul in Romans 12:1. It means "reasonable" or "rational" worship. Benedict describes it as "worship shaped by the word, structured on reason". It is closely associated with the patristic notion of *thysía logikē* (spiritual sacrifices or "sacrifices after the manner of the word").

Lohfink, Gerhard. German Catholic priest and New Testament scholar (1934–present).

Lüdemann, Gerd. German New Testament scholar (b. 1946) who denies the historicity of most of what is written in the Gospels, including the Resurrection accounts.

Maranatha. An Aramaic expression meaning "Our Lord, come!" or possibly "Our Lord has come." It is found transliterated into Greek in 1 Corinthians 16:22. The early Christians used the expression in the eucharistic liturgy, to emphasize Jesus' presence with his people. They also used it in supplication for, or in anticipation of, the second coming of Jesus.

Maximus the Confessor. Church Father and Byzantine theologian (A.D. 580–662) known best for his outspoken opposition to monothelitism, a heresy that claimed Christ had a divine will but not a human will. According to Maximus, Jesus' agony in Gethsemane is inexplicable unless he possessed a human will that could yield itself to the Father's will. Though exiled and tortured for his insistence on this point, Maximus was eventually vindicated by the Sixth Ecumenical Council (Constantinople III, A.D. 680), which defined that the incarnate Son had two wills, one human and one divine. Pope Benedict draws upon the insights of Maximus in his treatment of Jesus' prayer in Gethsemane.

Meier, John P. A biblical scholar and Catholic priest. He is perhaps best known for his historical-critical multivolume work on the historical Jesus called *A Marginal Jew*. The premise of his critical work is that he proceeds using a critical method, the results of which he maintains might produce agreement about Jesus of Nazareth's identity and intentions among critical Catholic, Protestant, Jewish, and agnostic scholars.

Melchisedek. The king of Salem identified in Genesis 14:18 as "priest of God Most High" to whom Abram offers a tithe. The Letter to the Hebrews, citing Psalm 110:4, speaks of Christ as belonging to the priesthood according to "the order of Melchizedek" (Heb 7:17). Pope Benedict, following the Jesuit biblical scholar Albert Cardinal Vanhoye, stresses Jesus' obedient yes in the Garden of Gethsemane to the Father's will as "consecrating" Jesus as a priest "according to the order of Melchisedek", as opposed to the priesthood possessed by descendants of Aaron.

Menke, Karl-Heinz. A German Catholic priest and theologian (b. 1950). He is a professor of dogmatic theology at the Catholic Theological Faculty of the University of Bonn.

Messori, Vittorio. Contemporary Italian journalist and author of a book on the Passion and death of Jesus Christ called *Patì sotto Ponzio Pilato?* (*He suffered under Pontius Pilate?*). Pope Benedict refers to Messori's thesis that Jesus acted according to the Law when he cleansed the Jerusalem Temple.

Misericordia. Latin word for "mercy".

Mishnah. A written compilation of Jewish oral tradition assembled in Palestine under Rabbi Judah the Prince (ca. A.D. 200). Its teachings are grouped into six main categories or "orders", each of which is subdivided into treatises or "tractates".

Mittelstaedt, Alexander. Author of an important study in German, *Lukas als Historiker*, that maintains that both the Gospel of Luke and the Acts of the Apostles were written before the fall of Jerusalem in A.D. 70.

Money-changers. Mentioned in the Gospels as those who exchanged foreign currency for the required Tyrian coins that Jewish pilgrims needed to pay the annual Temple tax. Jesus angrily overturned their tables when he discovered such business dealings taking place within the precincts of the sanctuary, probably in the outer Court of the Gentiles (Mt 21:12; Mk 11:15; Jn 2:14–15).

Monophysitism. The view that Christ had only one nature, in which his humanity had been absorbed into his divinity. Catholic, Orthodox, and traditional Protestant Christianity maintains that Christ possessed a fully human and a fully divine nature. The term "monophysitism" comes from two Greek terms: *mono*, meaning "one", and *physis*, meaning "nature".

Monothelitism. The view that Christ had only one will. Catholic, Orthodox, and traditional Protestant Christianity affirm that Christ possessed both a human and a divine will. The term "monothelitism" comes from two Greek terms: *mono*, meaning "one", and *thelelis*, meaning "will".

Mount of Olives. Mount that rises directly east of Jerusalem and is separated from the city by the Kidron Valley. Gethsemane, the garden where Jesus prayed in agony after the Last Supper, was part of an ancient farmstead on the lower slopes of the mount where olives were harvested and pressed into oil (Mt 26:30, 36). The Gospels indicate that Jesus often spent time there with his disciples (Lk 22:39; Jn 18:1–2).

Mussner, Franz. A German theologian and biblical scholar (1916–present).

Ne plus ultra. Latin expression meaning "not more beyond". Benedict uses it in connection with the evangelist's statement that Jesus loved his disciples "to the end" (Jn 13:1). The idea is that Christ loved them to the extreme limit, even to the point of sacrificing his life (cf. Jn 15:13).

Nestorians. Advocates of the view of Nestorius, a fifth-century bishop who taught that in Christ there were two distinct persons, one human and one divine, who were united only by the perfect agreement of their wills. Nestorianism was rejected by the Council of Ephesus in 431.

New commandment. Jesus' commandment given to his disciples at the Last Supper and referred to in John 13:34–35. Jesus said, "A new commandment I give to you, that you love one another; even as I have loved you, that you also love one another.

By this all men will know that you are my disciples, if you love one another." Benedict stresses that it is not simply a higher moral standard or greater moral accomplishment that makes the commandment new, but a new foundation—the gift of being-*with* and being-*in* Christ.

Ochlos. Greek word meaning "crowd" or "mob". Pope Benedict discusses the term's meaning in relation to the crowd who sought the death of Jesus.

Ontological. Having to do with the *being* of a thing or a person.

Palm Sunday. Christian feast that always falls on the Sunday before Easter. It commemorates Jesus' entry into Jerusalem (Mt 21:1–11; Mk 11:1–11; Lk 19:28–40; Jn 12:12–19) at the beginning of the final week of his earthly life.

Pannenberg, Wolfhart. A German Protestant theologian (b. 1928) whose work on Christology stresses the historical reality of Jesus' Resurrection.

Pascal, Blaise. French Catholic mathematician, scientist, and philosopher (1623–1662). Pascal is considered a pioneer in the development of probability theory and was the author of several important works, including a defense of Christianity called *Pensées*.

Passover. Jewish feast commemorating the Exodus of the Israelites from Egypt (see Ex 12:1–20; Lev 23:5; Deut 16:1–8, 12). Jesus' bread of life discourse (Jn 6:1–51), the Last Supper (Jn 12:1; 13:1–2, 21–28), and Jesus' death occur during or near the time of the Passover. Scholars debate whether Jesus died on the Passover or on the day of preparation, before the Passover. Pope Benedict favors the latter view, which is the position presented in the Gospel of John.

Pax Romana. Latin for "Roman Peace". This refers to the era of relative stability and peace that spanned the Roman world from the beginning of the reign of Caesar Augustus in 27 B.C. until the First Jewish War against the Romans that broke out in Palestine in A.D. 66. Governors appointed by Rome were charged with maintaining this peace by a strict enforcement of Roman law and, when necessary, the threat of military force.

Pesch, Rudolf. German biblical scholar whose scholarship points to the Jewish sources of John's Gospel.

Peterson, Erik. German theologian and Catholic convert from Lutheranism (1890–1960). He wrote on early Christianity as well as on subjects such as political theology and systematics.

Pharisees. Jewish movement, founded after the Babylonian exile, known for its strict adherence to the laws and regulations of the Torah. In Jesus' time and before, the Pharisees strongly resisted the Hellenistic and Roman influence on Jewish life. The Pharisees often opposed the Sadducees, another group within Judaism. After the destruction of the Second Temple in A.D. 70, Pharisaic theology became the basis for rabbinic Judaism. Jesus frequently disputed with the Pharisees.

Philo of Alexandria. First-century Jewish philosopher and theologian from Alexandria, Egypt (ca. 20 B.C.–A.D. 50). Philo attempted an exposition of the Jewish faith by means of the concepts and categories of Greek philosophy.

Pilate, Pontius. Prefect of the Roman province of Judea between A.D. 26 and A.D. 36, Pilate was the Roman official in charge of the execution of Jesus. At the end of his reign, Pilate was removed for his brutality by the Roman emperor. Pilate is present in all four Gospel accounts (Mt 27:1–26; Mk 15:1–15; Lk 23:1–15; Jn 18:28–19:16).

Plato. Classical Greek philosopher (429–347 B.C.). He was a student of Socrates, a teacher of Aristotle, and the author of many influential works, including *The Republic*. His ideas were later adapted by Plotinus, the founder of Neoplatonism.

Platonic philosophies. Philosophical systems derived from Plato or his followers.

Plotinus. Ancient philosopher (ca. A.D. 205–270) generally regarded as the founder of Neoplatonism, a development of the system of philosophy based on the ideas of the Greek philosopher Plato. He taught a form of the doctrine of *exitus* and *reditus*. Benedict contrasts Plotinus' doctrine with the Gospel of John's teaching about Jesus' "coming from" (*exitus*) and "returning to" (*reditus*) the Father.

Post factum. Latin expression meaning "after the deed" or "after the fact".

Praetorium. Latin name for the official residence of a Roman provincial governor. There were two praetorian palaces in Judea in the first century, one in Caesarea (Acts 23:35) and one in Jerusalem (Mk 15:16). The latter is where Jesus was taken by Jewish authorities (Jn 18:28) to be examined by Pontius Pilate (Jn 18:33; 19:9).

Prologue of John's Gospel. John 1:1–18

Qumran. Site of the discovery of the Dead Sea Scrolls. Located near the northwest corner of the Dead Sea, it was the dwelling place of the Essenes, a Jewish sect opposed to worship in the Herodean Temple in Jerusalem. There are some indications that John the Baptist and perhaps Jesus and his family may have had some association with this community, though the teaching of John and of Jesus differed significantly from that of the Qumran community.

Redaction criticism. A method of studying texts that seeks to understand how authors or editors have selected or shaped the material they have put into their texts.

Regula fidei. Latin phrase meaning "rule of faith". The term refers to a short summary of the essential content of the Christian faith, linked to confessions of faith (creeds) used in Baptism. Benedict, along with many other scholars, sees such a rule of faith as the key to unlocking the interpretation of Scripture, according to Scripture's own spirit.

Reiser, Marius. Catholic theologian and philologist (b. 1954) to whose work Pope Benedict refers as an important contribution to new ways of interpreting the Bible.

Resurrection of Jesus. The entrance by Jesus, following his death on the Cross, into an entirely new form of life that lies beyond the order of natural biological generation (Mt 22:30), resuscitation, and dying (1 Cor 15:42–44) and that includes a transformed bodily dimension of existence (1 Cor 15:50–54), possessing physical (Lk 24:39; Jn 20:24–27) and spiritual (Lk 24:31; Jn 20:19) aspects. The Resurrection is the Father's vindication of Jesus' divine sonship (Acts 2:24; Rom 1:4) and validation of the believer's faith in Jesus' redemption of sinful humanity (1 Cor 15:14, 17). It is also the pledge or "first fruits" of a general resurrection of the righteous (1 Cor 15:23), the beginning of a new kind of humanity to be realized in the age to come. The Resurrection of Jesus is not the mere passing of a spirit into the next life or a miraculous resuscitation to mortal existence, as with Lazarus. It is an entirely new mode of bodily existence.

Ringleben, Joachim. A German Lutheran theologian (b. 1945) whose book *Jesus* (2008) Benedict sees as an ecumenical compliment to his own volumes on Jesus of Nazareth.

Rupert of Deutz. Benedictine monk, theologian, and Scripture scholar (1075–1129). He was a commentator on John's Gospel and developed the theme of Jesus as high priest who both offered the atoning sacrifice and who was himself the sacrifice offered.

Sacramentum. Latin term for "sacrament", which Catholic teaching defines as an outward sign and instrument of grace. Ordinarily it refers to one of the seven sacraments of the Church. However, the term is sometimes used more broadly with reference to the Church herself as the sacrament of salvation for the world (for example, see Vatican II, *Lumen Gentium*, 1) or more generally to the mysteries of the life of Jesus. Benedict uses *sacramentum* in the last sense.

Sacramentum futuri. Latin term used for the idea, held by some Church Fathers, that animal sacrifices and other elements of the Old Testament pointed toward, and received dignity from, the sacrifice of Christ; also in certain ways anticipated the sacraments of the Church.

Sadducees. Jewish sect founded in the second century B.C., known for its denial of the afterlife, including the resurrection from the dead. The Sadducees at the time of Jesus were committed to the integration of Hellenism and Judaism, and they attempted to make the best of Roman rule. They often opposed the Pharisees, but were generally united with them in opposition to Jesus.

Sanctification. Term referring to an act of consecration or process of making some-thing or someone holy. It can mean "to render fit for divine worship". Sanctification generally involves "setting apart" something or someone for ordinary life or use and dedicating it to divine service. What is sanctified then mediates the divine to the world. As Benedict observes, in John's Gospel there is a triple "sanctification": the sanctification of the Son by the Father, who sends him into the world (Jn 10:36); the self-sanctification, or dedication, of the Son, and the Son's prayer for the sanctification of his disciples (Jn 17:17, 19).

Sanhedrin. The assembly (Greek, *synedrion*, "assembly") of Jewish leaders. In this context, it refers to the Council of Jewish leaders in Jerusalem who condemned Jesus to death for blasphemy and who turned him over to the Romans for execu-tion for sedition.

Scapegoat. One of two male goats featured in the ancient Day of Atonement liturgy. One goat, chosen by lot, was sacrificed to the Lord as a sin-offering; the other, which came to be known as the scapegoat, was designated to bear the sins of Israel into the wilderness (Lev 16:7–10). According to the rite, the high priest confessed the iniquities of the people over the animal and symbolically placed their trans-gressions upon its head before banishing it to a barren land (Lev 16:20–22).

Schnackenburg, Rudolf. German Catholic biblical exegete (1914–2002) who attempted to correct some of what he saw as the imbalances of historical-critical scholarship in order to support the Catholic faithful. Pope Benedict agrees with his basic goal but not with particular elements of his interpretations.

Schönborn, Christoph Cardinal. Catholic Dominican theologian and archbishop of Vienna, Austria (b. 1945); primary editor of the *Catechism of the Catholic Church*. Pope Benedict refers to Cardinal Schönborn's Christological work.

Schürmann, Heinz. Contemporary Catholic New Testament scholar and author of a collection of essays in German entitled *Jesus: Gestalt und Geheimnis* (*Jesus: Shape and Mystery* [1994]). He describes Jesus as leading a "pro-existence"—a life lived for others (the Latin *pro* meaning "for" or "on behalf of").

Schwemer, Anna Maria. Contemporary German scholar (b. 1942) and collaborator with Martin Hengel on an important study called *Jesus und das Judentum* (*Jesus and Judaism* [2007]). Benedict relies on this scholarly work at several points in his book.

Seewann, Maria-Irma. Contemporary German scholar and coauthor with Norbert Baumert, S.J., of an important article on the meaning of Jesus' words at the Last Supper (*Gregorianum* 89 [2008]).

Servant Songs. The name given to four poems in the Book of Isaiah that describe the "servant" of Yahweh (Is 42:1–9; 49:1–7; 50:4–11; 52:13—53:12). This mysterious figure is closely identified with Israel (Is 49:3), yet his mission is to bring salvation to Israel and the nations alike (Is 42:1; 49:6). Most striking is the revelation that redemption will come through the servant's bitter experience of suffering and death (Is 50:6; 53:3–12). Christian tradition from earliest times sees the fulfillment of these visions in Jesus as the suffering and saving Messiah.

Söding, Thomas. German Catholic theologian, New Testament scholar (b. 1956), and author of several studies that Benedict relies upon in the course of his book.

Solomon. Son and successor of David as king of a united Israel. Solomon's reign from ca. 970 to 930 B.C. was a political high point in the history of the chosen people.

Son of David. Originally a reference to Solomon, the royal son and successor of David, but eventually used as title for David's most illustrious descendant, the Messiah.

Son of Man. Title used by Jesus for himself and only rarely by others with respect to Jesus (see Acts 7:56). It has strong roots in the Old Testament, especially in the Book of Daniel (7:13–14). The figure of the Son of Man in Daniel shares in the authority of God, the Ancient of Days. Jesus uses the expression in this way to indicate his divine authority, not merely his human nature.

Stöger, Alois. German New Testament scholar. Benedict refers to his two-volume commentary on the Gospel of Luke (1969).

Studer, Basil. Benedictine theologian and patristics scholar (1925–2008).

Stuhlmacher, Peter. German Protestant theologian and New Testament scholar (b. 1926) who has written major works on Jesus and Christian origins.

Suffering Servant. A tragic figure whose rejection and violent abuse are graphically depicted in two of Isaiah's poems, called the third and fourth Servant Songs (Is 50:4–11; 52:13—53:12). Because his suffering and demise are portrayed by the Prophet as acts of redemption for sinners, Christian interpretation going back to New Testament times identified the Suffering Servant with Jesus Christ (see Mt 8:17; Lk 22:37; Acts 8:32–35).

Suffering Servant Songs. Songs concerning the figure of the Suffering Servant (Is 50:4–11; 52:13—53:12). Christian interpretation applies the songs to Jesus.

Synoptics (Synoptic Gospels). The Gospels of Matthew, Mark, and Luke. They are called "synoptic" Gospels because of their similar structures and use of much of the same material to narrate Christ's works and teachings. "Synoptic" means "same view" or "view together".

Teresa of Avila, Saint. Spanish mystic, Carmelite nun, and Doctor of the Church (1515–1582). Teresa worked tirelessly with John of the Cross as a reformer of the Carmelite Order; she was also a profound spiritual writer, with several classics to her credit, including *The Way of Perfection*.

Tertullian. Early Latin theologian and apologist from Carthage in North Africa (ca. A.D. 160–225).

Tetélestai. Greek word translated as "It is finished", and the final expression of the dying Jesus in John 19:30. It expresses Jesus' total gift of himself in loving his disciples "to the end" (*télos*; Jn 13:1) and accomplishing the mission entrusted to him by the Father (Jn 4:34; 5:36; 17:4).

Theophanies. Manifestations of God's presence in the concrete world of history and human experience. Benedict compares certain features of Old Testament theophanies with the Gospel accounts of the Resurrection.

Thomas Aquinas, Saint. Italian saint and Dominican theologian and philosopher (1225–1274). He is called the Angelic Doctor and is highly regarded in the Catholic theological tradition. Two of his major works are the *Summa Theologiae* and the *Summa Contra Gentiles*. Pope Benedict likens his approach in his books on Jesus of Nazareth to the theological reflections of the *Summa Theologiae* on the mysteries of Christ's life.

Thysía logikē. Greek term used by the Greek Fathers of the Church to refer to "spiritual sacrifices" as opposed to animal sacrifices, which they regarded as obsolete. With the coming of Jesus and the demise of the Temple, animal sacrifices are replaced by "spiritual sacrifices".

Times of the Gentiles. A period of time referred to explicitly by Jesus in Luke's account of the eschatological discourse. Jesus says that Jerusalem will be trodden down "until the times of the Gentiles are fulfilled" (Lk 21:24). Some scholars claim that Luke, not Jesus, introduced this idea in order to allow for an "age of the Church" to precede the end of the world. Benedict shows how the other Synoptic evangelists implicitly include the "times of the Gentiles" in their accounts of Jesus' eschatological discourse (Mt 24:14; Mk 13:10), as well as elsewhere (Mt 13:24–30, 47–50). Jesus anticipated such a period in which his teaching would be spread to the nations (Mt 28:19).

Titus. Son of the emperor Vespasian and commander of the Roman forces that quelled the first Jewish revolt and conquered Jerusalem in A.D. 70. Titus succeeded his father as emperor in A.D. 79.

Torah. Refers generally to the Law of Moses and specifically to the Pentateuch, the first five books of the Hebrew Scriptures, or Old Testament: Genesis, Exodus, Leviticus, Numbers, and Deuteronomy.

Tradition criticism. A method of biblical research that attempts to understand how biblical authors used earlier biblical traditions and other, non-biblical traditions.

Trōgein. Greek verb "to eat", a form of which is used in John's account of Jesus' "bread of life" discourse to refer to the necessity of "eating" his flesh—that is, receiving the Eucharist (Jn 6:54–58). In John's account of the Last Supper, Jesus uses a form of *trōgein* when he quotes Psalm 41:9 to refer to his betrayal by Judas, thus linking Judas' act to abuse of the Eucharist.

Twelve, the. A special group of disciples chosen by Jesus and given special authority in the community of his disciples. They are sometimes called the twelve Apostles (Lk 6:13), although the term "Apostle" can extend to a wider category of leaders who witnessed the Resurrection of Jesus (1 Cor 15:8). The Twelve represent the spiritual foundation of the new Israel of the Church as the old Israel was made up of the biological foundation of the twelve tribes.

Vanhoye, Albert Cardinal. Jesuit biblical scholar and leading expert on the interpretation of the Letter to the Hebrews (b. 1923). He was a longtime professor at the Pontifical Biblical Institute in Rome until his retirement in 1998. Vanhoye was made a cardinal by Pope Benedict in 2006.

Via dolorosa. Latin expression meaning "sorrowful way". Benedict uses it as a synonym for the whole Passion of Jesus from Gethsemane to Golgotha. *Via Dolorosa* is also the name given to a traditional route in Jerusalem where Christian pilgrims walk and pray the Stations of the Cross. The present route begins near the Ecce Homo Arch (in the Muslim Quarter) and ends inside the Church of the Holy Sepulcher (in the Christian Quarter).

Vicarious atonement. A theological concept used to explain the redemptive work of Christ. It denotes how a representative substitute (Jesus) stands in for sinners (the human family) in order to reconcile them with God and reestablish justice.

Vox populi. Latin for "the voice of the people". In Roman society, ordinary persons had the right to voice their opinions and concerns on matters related to government administration. Benedict sees this democratic principle at work in the shouts of the crowd assembled before Pontius Pilate (see Mk 15:8–14).

Wilckens, Ulrich. Contemporary German Lutheran bishop and New Testament scholar (b. 1928) who has argued that the beloved disciple in John's Gospel was not a historical figure but a symbol. Pope Benedict rejects his view as incompatible with the Gospel of John's presentation of the beloved disciple as an eyewitness of the events it describes.

Yom Kippur. Hebrew expression meaning "day of atonement", which is the English term for the corresponding Jewish feast.

Zealot. A member of the militantly anti-Roman Jewish sect that lived and agitated in Palestine from at least the mid-first century B.C. until it was annihilated during the Roman destruction of the Jewish rebellion, ca. A.D. 70. At least one of the Twelve, Simon, called the Zealot, seems at some point to have been a Zealot sympathizer (Lk 6:15).

Zōē. A Greek word meaning "life". "*Zōē*" is used by Jesus in John's Gospel to refer to "eternal life", "true" life that death cannot overcome. It is obtained through recognizing the true God and the one he has sent, Jesus Christ (Jn 17:3). *Zōē* stands in contrast with mere biological life (*bios*).